DON'T LOOK A GIFT COUCH IN THE MOUTH

Guffawfully Fun Stories from the World of Animals and Rescue

TAMIRA THAYNE
AND OTHER SPECIAL GUEST AUTHORS

Published by FreedomChaser Books
www.fcanimalbooks.com

Written, edited, and designed by
Tamira Thayne

Cover Illustration by Rocky Shepheard

Paperback ISBN: 978-1-954039-72-8

Printed in the United States of America

First Edition

To Joe

For putting up with me all these years.

& To You

For putting up with me for five seconds.

But stick with me for a bit.

I trust these pages will bring you a smile,
a chuckle, or even a guffaw or two.

For the Animals!

Also Available from Tamira Thayne

Rescue Smiles

More Rescue Smiles

Unchain My Heart

It Went to the Dogs

Capitol in Chains

Foster Doggie Insanity

The Wrath of Dog

The King's Tether

The Knight's Chain

The Curse of Cur

Smidgey Pidgey's Predicament

Raffy Calfy's Rescue

Spittin' Kitten's Speedaway

Squirmy Hermie's Heroics

No Guppy Puppy

Welcome. Put Up Your Feet. Stay Awhile.

Laughs in animal rescue? Few and far between . . . but the heartbreaks come fast and furious, so we're declaring a moratorium on sadness for as long as you're with us today.

Come in, prop up your feet, drop a chuckle or two, and toss your troubles in a nearby doody bag.

Enjoy a laugh at our expense.

After all, the air is rank with the stank of doo, the floors are awash in muddy gloop, and dinner coagulates on the back burner.

But you are far, far away in your imaginary castle, kicking back on your own possibly-shredded couch, and happy for these few and far between crumbs of contentment.

Enjoy. Giggle. Titter. Belly laugh. Amaze yourself at our insanity, audacity, or indescribably bad taste.

And then jump up refreshed, ready to tackle today's personal struggle, convinced (for one incandescent moment) that everything will be ok.

Ha! That last laugh might be on you...

Yay, You're Here, You're Here!

Welcome...

Table of Contents

Double Doody?

January 2015
Value Size
7 LBS
330+ Treats
Hold On, Just Checkin'
My Bank Balance

These Beds
Used To Be
More
Comfortable

Don't Look a Gift Couch in the Mouth

BY TAMIRA THAYNE

My name is Tami, and I'm addicted to couch.

[You, in unison: Welcome, Tami.]

Most of the time, I don't even need them. [Denial, poor girl.]

In fact, I've had as many as two and a half couches, and only needed one in my living room which doubled as a doggy daycare and an office. [Senseless bragging to distract you…but you're too smart for that.]

Truth be told, I'm always on the lookout for a sweet couch deal.

My hopeless addiction to couch began while I was fostering dogs for the nonprofit I founded from my Pennsylvania home, Dogs Deserve Better. The organization freed chained dogs and brought them into the home and family, encouraging action for forgotten pups all across the U.S and even the world over.

Keep in mind, though, that these dogs weren't just ANY foster dogs, but the super-duper MEGA kind—the motherload of foster dogs. Because these were formerly chained or penned foster dogs. OUTSIDE DOGS. That's right. Outside dogs that I—apparently with NO respect for the natural order of things—turned around and dragged INSIDE.

You see, I've never believed that such a thing as an OUTSIDE dog EXISTS. Yes, I know there are technically dogs that spend their entire lives outdoors. . . .

But they're just dogs—normal, everyday dogs of all breeds and sizes—that a certain type of human banishes to the backyard like a sack of trash, meant to co-exist alongside such items as rusty washing machines, old tires, car skeletons, and the sound of banjo music.

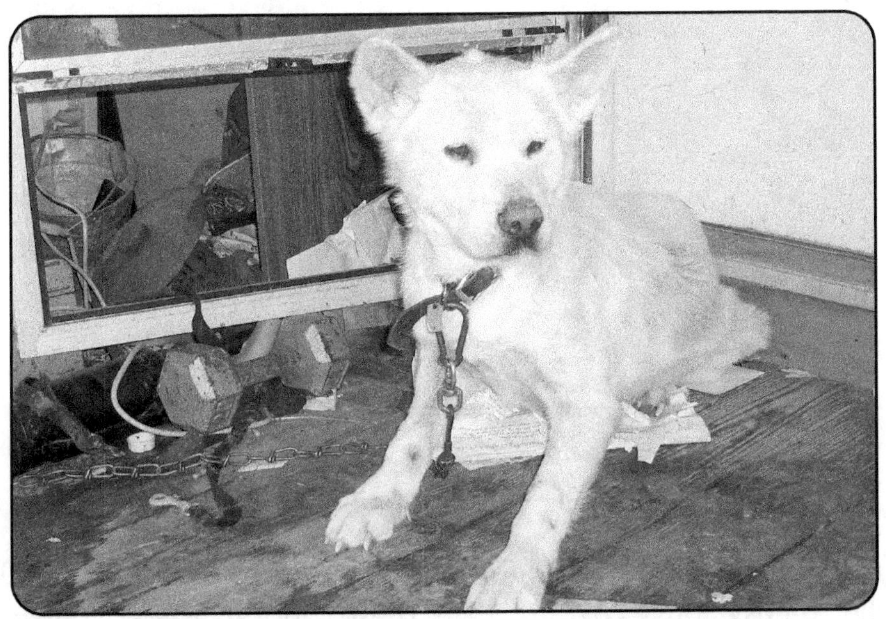

Not much funny about dog chaining, though, eh? Don't worry...
Ming is one of the three dogs sleeping on the couch in the pic, opposite page

I believe these folks call them OUTSIDE dogs to make themselves feel better about their ill-advised and ill-thought-out intentions. In fact, they've ill-defined these dogs, and I'm ill-disposed to tolerate it. I wish it were illegal everywhere to chain these illustrious dogs, and the very thought of it puts me in an ill humor.

So I, by rescuing these OUTSIDE dogs—in a super-fast twist of fate—turned them into INSIDE dogs, just like that. "Voila!" [Waves magic wand.] "I now proclaim you an INSIDE dog."

Poof.

Brandy left pawprints on hearts AND couches.

While this was theoretically all well and good, I was left with the teensy tinsy truism that these adorable—yet oh-so-stanky—dogs were not acquainted with life inside the home.

Thus, our adventures together often began in quite an ill-mannered fashion. Not their fault, of course; the blame lay with the ill-bred humans who banished them to the backyard without a lick of training in the first place.

Shortly after I, with much fanfare and how-dee-do, escorted these soon-to-be princes and princesses into my home, the males in particular would take to an insane obsession with my couch . . . and not in a good way.

They'd eye-ball said couch from across the room: "Hark, what manner of jewel doth mine eyes behold . . . could it be a lusciously soft place to rest my weariest-of-noggins? What sorceress hath created this haven placed high above the ground, wherein I may be crowned king?"

"To mine eyes, might this accordingly be more like a throne, perhaps? Yes, yes, a throne! And mayhap said throne can be of use to mine self in more ways than one…."

[And…Scene.]

No, I am KING of the couch mountain!

For, you see, the princes among the species, the OUTSIDE-turned-INSIDE dogs, were predisposed to use this glorious throne as a—well—THRONE, as well!

They'd measure it: "Yes, yes, the perfect height . . . perfect length for more than one spritz . . . in fact, I'm pretty sure I can garnish this thing in both corners AND the middle with just one—prolonged-and-appropriately-aimed—squirt."

Sniffing: "Indeed. No one shall ever again doubt this is MY territory. For I, the Prince of the OUTSIDE-turned-INSIDE dogs, have marked it as my own. And so it shall be. Furever and ever. Amen."

Not only did the sprinkler system go off repeatedly with the arrival of each new Prince, but their enthrallment with the couch didn't end there. No sir-ee. Turns out couches are great roll zones, bone-burying spots, wrestling match arenas, scratching posts, and gnawing sites, too.

You might be bigger, Beast, but this is MY toy!

Over my years in the foster game I owned more couches than I can possibly recollect. My one-time boyfriend, Rocky— while he was still my boyfriend—managed to finagle us an "in" with a local furniture company. They twice donated used-but-still-in-great-shape couches that they'd removed from homes where they'd delivered an upgrade.

Sweet Lord-in-Heaven! These "reject couches" from others were my bounty, a precious gem to be treasured for that brief moment in time before they were christened and hence befouled by my foster dogs.

*Dusty was a 99.99% on the cuteness scale during his couch time with us.
We can now reveal his housetraining score was a tad lower.*

Then the company went out of business—I swear in no part due to Dogs Deserve Better—and my visions of a life-long couch-drug supply dried up with it.

In a state of panic, I began hoarding what couches I was able to get my greedy little paws on. I slathered them with blankets, which were removed and washed daily or when the goo or sprinkler system got out of control. These countermeasures elongated the life-cycle of each couch, but always in the end the disgust-o-meter became too high and the damage beyond repair—I just had to get my hands on a new couch!

There was even a time—gasp—when I was entirely couch-less, and was forced by circumstances beyond my control to scour the neighborhood for a new doggy-lounger.

Of course, only the most high-falutin yard sale couch would do; there was zero point to paying for a pre-destroyed one…I had standards to uphold, after all! I'd begun to despair when Rocky and I were driving a country road one day and spotted it: no, not a couch, per se, but more like an extra large overstuffed chair with a bonus ottoman. Score!

Delilah gave the oversized-chair her grin of approval.

It wasn't the perfect solution, but since I hate yard sales and shopping altogether—and this one would fit into the back of my van—I pronounced it sufficiently adequate, something any would-be couch aspires to. Rocky talked them down to $45, we weakling-handled it into the back of the vehicle, and the throne-room was back in business, baby!

Then something bizarre happened.

In an unforeseen plot twist, due to its smaller size or the fact that I had covered it so proficiently [pats herself on the back,] the not-perfect, overgrown, not-quite-a-couch chair survived my dog-infested house for MONTHS, closer to a YEAR. It was unheard of!

I couldn't get rid of it! It was in too good-a shape!

I found myself fruitlessly fantasizing about its sure-to-be-forthcoming destruction. *Should I cover it in Milkbones?*

I plotted and obsessed. It gradually dawned on me that I might have a little problem: *could I, would I, have become addicted to couch through this little rescue experiment?*

Who let the wolf in? Wolves deserve better too! Ohoyo was a wolf hybrid who was abandoned by her family and jumped over a balcony to free herself.

The final nail in my evidence-coffin came when my boyfriend Joe downsized from his house into an apartment, and asked me if I wanted his futon couch.

I lusted. I couldn't say no, even though that damn not-perfect overgrown chair was still alive.

Who knew when another such opportunity might come along?

Jack's first in line to chow down on the new futon frame.
"That's some pristine couch proppity; don't mind if I do."

Joe's futon had a beautiful wooden frame (perfect for gnawing) and a cloth cushion, just ripe for the ripping. I could see my donated blankets gracing its bones now.

Oh, yes.

I rearranged and rearranged to squeeze the futon into my living room with the chair that wouldn't die.

I now had TWO covered thrones for my kingly guests.

I celebrated my good luck, need for a hit of couch all but sated...

UNTIL, as luck would have it, my friends Terri and Eric were staging their house for sale. They asked if I wanted a half-shredded couch that their cats were diligently working on. Both edges were all but destroyed, but they insisted there was still life in it.

Note the ripped edging, but Puppy Pete was still a fan.

Hell, yeah, just what I'd been looking for!

So I moved the still-in-good-shape futon down to the garage-turned-headquarters with the DDB office manager, and the new, half-shredded couch to the upstairs with the not-dead chair.

It wasn't long before Terri and Eric's contribution was well-spritzed and well-soiled, courtesy of five princes in a row.

I anxiously renewed my vow to foster only female dogs—at least they had the courtesy to squat right in the middle of the floor—and began to keep an eye out for my next fix. . . .

"You're not bringing another dog in again, are you? I just claimed this chair!"

While it's been years since I've actively doggy-fostered, and I no longer (overtly) obsess over couches, I've found that the addiction still lurks, waiting for that first triggering mention of some new digs.

I recently overheard my husband Joe talking to his sister Ibi on the phone. "No," he said, "both boys have L-shaped couches in their living rooms, so they're good. Thanks for the offer, though."

He got off the phone to find himself the recipient of my best glare. "Did your sister just offer you a couch and you turned it down?"

My brain was already scrambling, picturing our current couch with the two-sided tape Joe'd plastered along the edges to keep the cats from destroying it. [Spoiler: yes, this looks WAY WORSE than anything our felines could accomplish.]

I felt dizzy. *He turned down a free couch? Without even consulting ME? Imma need to sit down.* It would seem that, even years later, a free new-used couch was nothing if not a prime delicacy.

"No, it was a couch, a loveseat, and two recliners she was offering . . . but they're white, which would be a total disaster here with the cats and the dog."

My mind was whirling. I felt like I might possibly swoon. "Recliners, you say?"

I can make that work.

"Call her back."

The author, daring to sit on her own couch, with foster dog Levi.

I'm just a dog, pretending to be human, talking to the staypuff-marshmallow-man who currently resides in my mouth. Nothing to see here.

Duck, Duck, Goose

BY MARTHA MOSLEY

Shupka with his friend Bupka

Our crates trailed straw across the veterinary office floor, the noise carrying with it an unexpectedly bittersweet feeling. Shupka had been captured.

In the spring, three Pekin ducks had been dumped at the little man-made lake in our retirement community. That lake, with its sandy beaches, picnic tables, and plentiful seating, is the go-to meeting place for many local residents. The mysterious appearance of three white ducks quickly became cause for excitement, speculation, and discussion.

Our township officials were not pleased. A considerable amount of funding had been spent the previous summer to hire the Geese Police, a company with border collies who chased waterfowl and humanely annoyed them into leaving. Due to their efforts the lake was soon geese-free, and this new plot twist presented a conundrum.

If people fed the new ducks, the argument went that Canada geese would again flock to the lake. No one wanted to walk barefoot on beaches polluted by bird poop, and that, it was agreed, would be the result if the ducks stayed. After all, there were summer camps for kids and community events held at the lake, and dirty beaches would impact attendance.

The dog warden was called into service. Margaret is a kind woman who is willing to attempt any task, and the first two ducks easily stepped into the trap she set. The third one would not.

After several days spent on the beach with various enclosures and traps, Margaret finally devised what she believed was a foolproof plan. She returned with the two ducks she had previously captured, set up a chicken wire enclosure around a wooden bench, and waited for the elusive fowl to come greet his friends. She could just close the wire behind him and he would be hers!

Instead, the duck waddled up the beach, greeted his old friends from a safe distance, and seemed to call, "Oh, hey guys, I wondered where you got to. Look at me . . . I'M LIVING MY VERY BEST LIFE!" Then he ran back to the water as fast as his little webbed feet would carry him, and Margaret was left speechless on the shore.

Many of us have a secret desire to rebel, and that ornery duck was doing just that. It was hard not to admire him! If his wings had fingers, there was no doubt that the middle one would have been standing straight up every time his would-be captors came near. Throughout the summer, that lone duck was the source of both entertainment and admiration for the community's animal lovers.

Autumn came, and with the cooler days fewer people visited the lake. Many of the residents packed up and escaped to their winter homes in Florida. As bad weather approached, there were only two people who remained consistently on "duck duty."

Elaine and Walter had not previously known one another, but they became a tag team, ensuring that the duck Elaine had named Shupka was fed twice a day. Even in the worst weather, footprints in the snow highlighted their dedication to their feathered friend.

Shupka spent his days hanging out with migrating Canada geese and huddling under the wooden dock at night. Beneath it, he was safer from predators, and—even if the rest of the lake froze over—the water under the dock would not.

The next spring, a nighttime secret mission brought Shupka a gift: another Pekin duck was released into the lake, and Shupka gained a new friend. The two became inseparable, eating, sleeping, and swimming side by side. Elaine, true to her Polish heritage, named this one Bupka.

The two ducks became local celebrities of a sort. Residents visited the town hall to plead their case and enumerate the pleasures they brought to visitors. An enclosure left on the beach as a shelter for them immediately disappeared, but otherwise township officials seemed to look the other way. The ducks' stay might be indefinite after all!

Shupka and Bupka, the local celebrities

But then the lake froze solid just before Christmas. Bupka had never adapted to life in the wild as well as his more adventurous companion. When he hurt his leg trying to walk on the ice, Margaret was asked for her help in the matter. The injured Bupka was easily captured and went along without protest to Margaret's house for rehabilitation.

Shupka was alone again.

The dock had needed repair and been removed the previous summer. Without that dock, Shupka had no place to hide and nowhere to shelter in inclement weather. Pekin ducks need at least a liter of water a day, and with the water frozen solid it was impossible for Shupka to get that. Water left out for him froze too quickly to prevent dehydration.

Despite all the difficulties, that stubborn boy still eluded capture. He spent Christmas on the frozen lake with a few geese friends, but two days later, Walter found Shupka huddled beneath a bush, eyes glazed. He was obviously in distress.

Elaine, wisely, had never tried to catch Shupka. Therefore, she was the one person he trusted. She arrived, approached him easily, and was able to lift the weakened duck into a dog crate.

An era had ended.

Shupka and Bupka were nursed back to health and then re-located to a farm where they are safe and cared-for. Elaine and Walter still visit, and the two ducks are always happy to see them. They have ducky girlfriends, plentiful food, and shelter in bad weather. It's likely they spend their evenings like old sailors, entertaining the others with tales of lives spent on the water and adventures in the wild.

As for the rest of us, when driving by the lake, we tend to slow down. We're wishing for one more glimpse of that feisty little duck; the one who tested limits, broke rules, and lived his very best life.

Martha Mosley has spent a lifetime enjoying animals of all types and rescuing those who need it. Her children's book, **A Place for Grace,** is available on Amazon and recognizes the value of the seasoned love that older dogs offer. She also has had stories published in the *Chicken Soup for the Soul* series.

Martha lives in New Jersey with her husband Howard and adult offspring Michelle and Andrew. Their household has three dogs: Gigi a pit mix, Ella a border collie mix, and Sasha a dachshund.

She spends time reading, gardening, volunteering and walking their dogs.

Methinks someone needs driving school.
Just sayin'.

Tootie the Camper Cat

BY TAMIRA THAYNE

The hubby Joe, yours truly, and my feral cat Tootie spent over a year at the end of the pandemic traveling the U.S. in search of freedom (not the cult kind), adventure (no mountain climbing for this girl), and any interesting animals and people we met along the way.

Since the three of us were freakishly shy, we met more animals than humans throughout our time on the road. Now that I think on it, we made not a single human friend on our entire journey. NerdsRUs.

But the animals, you might wonder? Well, those "friends" I make by awkwardly spying on them in the wild. Through the window. As one does.

So while I consider myself and every animal I watch besties, they hold a different opinion on the matter. "Tami who? Stop gaslighting me. I never met that nutter in my life!"

Before we could commence on our grand adventure, however, Joe dropped me and dear Tootance at my mother and stepfather's home in Bellwood, Pennsylvania, so I could make myself useful while he wound down his final month of work.

My mother suffered from advanced dementia, was no longer verbal, and unable to care for herself; her husband Chuck was determined that she wouldn't die alone in a nursing home, and so he struggled to keep her home with him.

While Tootie and I were helping out, she set up her own little commune under the bed. *I mean, what can you expect from a feral cat, anyway?* Tootie very much loved her mommy though, so she would gather her courage and bravely venture up onto the bed for some nighttime momma cuddles.

Her "stranger danger" kept her in hiding for most if not all relevant daylight hours. But after Mom and Chuck went to sleep? Party Tootie came out to play…or lay, as the case may be. *Whatevs.* At least she was out of the guest room!

When Joe arrived with the camper and set up at a nearby campground, we agreed to pick up Tootie the next evening, since we still had a lot of work to get the camper in order. And—to be honest—we were terrified of wrassling her out from under the bed.

My little tuxedo kitty was in a strange place, scared, and by nature wild. She'd bit me not too long before when I was trying to give her medication, so I held a pretty healthy respect for her general chomper zone and tended to avoid enraging that particular area.

I prayed to the gawds of all things cat that Tootie would eventually "get" what we were up to and docilely patter into the crate to be moved from the camper to the truck and back again on moving days. We were definitely not there yet.

The wrassling went as poorly as you could imagine, and included ferocious growling and gnashing of teeth. *Tootie wasn't happy either.* I was a little too fluffy to fit under the bed (eh-hem), so I had to scour the garage for a primitive cat-sweeping tool, finding a set of old crutches that would fit the bill.

I quickly learned that Tootie must have had a bad crutch experience in her kittenhood, because she immediately set to attacking the offending "cat sweepers" in a most unladylike manner.

The ensuing battle spilled from the bedroom into the laundry room, where after some more "persuasion" she was finally cornered and morosely slipped into her crate, pouting in the corner.

I would have taunted her for being such a sore loser about it all, but I preferred not to have my face ripped off in the middle of the night; hence, I wisely kept any commentary to myself.

Plus, I loved her. She was my little Tootie Monster, after all.

We Learned As We Went

The next few campgrounds proved to be similarly painful for our little family of three. On moving days, Joe and I chased and cornered my little angel, while Tootie hid, hissed, scratched, and bit. By the time we got on the road, the camper was in shambles and the mood was definitively less than party-like.

I eventually figured out that if we could convince Tootie the crate was her safe spot, we would have better luck moving her from the camper into the truck. Theoretically, she would run and hide in her crate when scared as opposed to some other crevasse she'd recently discovered.

So I set up her crate on the bedside stand next to me and she could go into "her room" and hide whenever she liked. *What a gamechanger!* Soon we were old pros at "capture the cat," and even Tootie started to enjoy herself on the trip.

She loved to sit at the screen door and watch the birds and other animals going about their business, mumbling to herself in quiet catspeak as she watched.

Tootie proved to be the perfect camper companion for us. Joe had no interest in a cat curling up in his lap or snuggling him in bed, and I had every interest in both of those things.

Tootie had no interest in men and clung to me instead, so the three of us quickly came to the best understanding possible: Mommy GETS all the kitty love and GIVES all the kitty love. Daddy provides assistance when needed but otherwise hangs out in his own recliner in his own bubble of space.

Just the way we liked it!

Road cat—as opposed to road kill— but just a little less grumpy.

The Lookalike Tootie

I remained terrified about misplacing Tootie on the trip, so we were super careful about ensuring doors were always shut and latched.

But there was this one time...

It had grown dark and Joe needed something from the truck. He opened the camper door only to find what appeared to be Tootie sitting on the stoop outside. He immediately whipped the door shut, looked about frantically, and said, "Where's Tootie?" in his most trepidatious is-my-wife-about-to-lose-her-schize voice.

"She's right there in her bed," I replied, jumping up and rushing the door. "Why, is there a cat outside?"

Yes. *Yes there was.* And while I remain skeptical of Joe's powers of animal observation, the resemblance, at first glance at least, was uncanny.

The Not-Tootie Tuxedo Kitty

This handsome tuxedo lad wanted in, was quite vocal about it, and really, who was I to un-oblige cat friends old or new?

I opened the door and invited him in.

"Tux" stepped one paw onto the welcome mat and realized he'd made a horrible error; this wasn't his house and these weren't his people! "I'm being catnapped," he panicked. "Run away, run away!"

He quickly pivoted and hightailed it back out the door, yet didn't go far; he simply hung around outside like he was lost and had nowhere to turn.

Craptastic. Did this mean I was going to have to talk to people in other campers, at NIGHT, on his behalf? It appeared so.

Doing a little muttering of my own, I dragged on a pair of flipflops and then clumsily traversed the camping neighborhood to knock on the doors of the closest campers, asking if anyone had lost a black and white tuxedo cat. No one fessed up. Eventually "Tux" took himself off toward the back of the campground and that was the end of our budding friendship.

I choose to believe he happily found his way home and I invite you to do the same. Tootie was disappointed that her doppelganger had fled without any parting gifts in the form of a good how-de-do sniff or whack from her.

Mayhaps you'll meet up with him at the Bridge, my sweet girl?

If so, send your mom pics. She misses you…oh so very much.

I Always Wanted a Doggie Door
...and Superman Eyes. Score!

Forty-Winks Plays Possum

BY JOSEPH HORVATH

When my wife, Tami, and I were dating, I would travel to her house in rural Pennsylvania to spend weekends or other days off with her. Because of her dog rescue work, she always had a house full of dogs, with fenced yards on both sides of the home and doggie doors leading inside through the downstairs office and her back porch.

Goodbyes were often hard, as I lived three hours away and we didn't know when our schedules would line up to see one another again. One evening I told her goodbye and got into my Durango to start the trip back to my job and apartment in northern Virginia. As I was backing out, Tami ran out of the house waving her arms to stop me.

My first thought was, "oh, she misses me already," but boy was I wrong!

I stopped and got out of my SUV, taking the opportunity to make dad jokes about her inability to live without me.

Like every woman, she loves a good dad joke.

She, however, wasn't laughing, or even pretending to laugh. She told me that one of the dogs had carried an opossum in through the doggie door in the office and she was laying deathly still on one of the dog beds. Tami wasn't sure if she was alive or dead.

I know that opossums are well known for their ability to faint and appear to be dead, so my initial impression upon viewing the opossum was one of uncertainty. She, who we promptly dubbed Forty Winks in hopes she was simply "taking a nap," definitely SEEMED to be unalive; careful, but gentle, prodding of her shoulder area produced no indication to the contrary.

We thought it best if I drove her a half-mile up the road and released her into the woods on the off-chance that she was still on this earthly plane. I carefully transferred her little body into a cat carrier and put the carrier into my vehicle.

Tami and I said our goodbyes again, but this time I bore an unexpected passenger who was possibly doing a bang-up job of faking her own death. I drove up the road a bit and stopped at the edge of a wooded area, peeking into the cat carrier. The opossum still hadn't moved an inch and appeared totally lifeless.

Cat carrier in hand, I walked over to the edge of the woods, lowered the carrier, and opened the door with it tilted slightly towards the ground. The opossum suddenly sprang to life, jumped out of the carrier, and unceremoniously waddled herself off into the woods.

I was pleased that Forty Winks had lived up to her impromptu alias and woken from her self-imposed nap, and I wished the now-vanishing creature a long (by opossum standards) life.

I also hoped she had learned a crucial life lesson that day: fences are there for a reason and often contain scary and potentially life-threatening beasts…canines who have zero qualms about carrying you off through a doggie door and into a faraway land.

Maybe just avoid the fence next time, Forty!

And you're welcome for the ride out of Dodge.

As a child of Hungarian immigrants, **Joseph Horvath** is a first-generation American who grew up in Pennsylvania and was immersed in the Hungarian culture until he joined the U.S. Air Force at the age of 18. He became a cryptologic linguist and later an imagery analyst until his retirement from the military.

Joseph is father to identical twin sons and became a grandfather in 2025. He holds a Master's degree in Geographic Information Systems and a Master's in Organizational Management. He continued his career supporting the U.S. Government for another 24 years before his final retirement in 2026.

Joseph enjoys hiking and traveling and has been to all 50 states and over 30 countries.

I'm here
about your car
insurance

Our Search for the Eloosive Moosive

BY TAMIRA THAYNE

New Englanders, and those who come for the beauty to be found in these illustriously-wooded states, are obsessed with the large land animal known as the **Eloosive Moosive.**

Not to be outdone, Joe and I decided to join in the fun, reasoning the meese had probably been waiting for us to come see them anyway. *Who were we to disappoint?*

Joe: I want to see a moose.

Me: Duh. We're in Mooseland. Of course we'll see a moose. Or even multiple meeses.

I was confident in our abilities, especially after the girl at the sub shop told us she'd seen TWO. *In one YEAR!*

Holy common AF. It goes without saying then that our task was to search out this mythical being.

Thus began our journey...

But There Was So Much "Fake Moos"

In order for us to lure him, her, or them (we're equal opportunity meese viewers) out into the open, we decided our best plan was to meander about pretending to do other things. *In their general vicinity.*

After all, we reasoned, this way we'd be sure to spot them from the corner of our eye and react accordingly. *Oooh…. aaaaahhhh….picture, picture, picture.*

Turns out meeses are sneaky bastages

To earn the favor of the moosegods, we even grabbed a site along the Moose River in Vermont, doubling down with our pick of the Moose River Campground. **Surely meeses abound here where they are immortalized in statue and signage, no?**

So We Searched LOW...

In bear caves

Under bridges

At dog parties

Among the rocks
And crevasses

...but zero moosei

We Went on Foot...And by Bike...

I even questioned a squirrel I trapped in a tree. "Every admission gets you one more peanut, bucko. *Now…where are the GD meeses? Are you acquainted with these beings? Take me to your moose leader.*"

But she just eyed me up and down dismissively, yanked the peanut out of my fingers, and escaped through the softly rustling leaves. *Turns out squirrels are sneaky bastages, too.* And able to withstand a measurable amount of torture by peanut. **Respect.**

And We Searched High...

I meant HIGH as in UP IN THE AIR, folks. Get your minds out of the cannabis gutter. *(I'll meet you there later…only where it's legal, of course, which it turns out is most of New England.)*

We hopped a cable car to the top of Cannon Mountain and a train to the top of Mt. Washington. The views made me glad I didn't scurry into hiding due to my fear of heights, but alas, once again not a single moosive was spotted.

In the end, I must report we were udder failures (see what I did there), without a single **Eloosive Moosive sighting to our names,** despite the diligence with which we undertook our mission.

Oh, we'll be back, Mooselandia. You shan't evade us a second time. To be continued…

Bayou Swamp
GATOR BURGER
PASS
N'AWLINS
GATOR
ON A STICK
HARD PASS
Louisiana
GATOR BITES
AW HAIL NO

Peter Rabbit's Second Wind

BY LINDA SHERMAN-KEDERSHA

When our daughter Marlaina was about six years old, we discovered a rabbit lying motionless at the bottom of our pool. This was, of course, not a great development for anyone involved, not the least of which was the poor bunny who had met his end in a way neither pleasant nor quick.

Marlaina, who firmly believed Mommy could fix anything, begged me to save his life and handed me the long-handled net so I could dredge him up and out of the pool. I saw no signs of a comeback for "Peter," but I dutifully retrieved a large cardboard box, put a soft towel inside, and gently laid the bunny upon it. Marlaina insisted we bring him inside the house so he wouldn't be alone while he "got better."

I kept my personal opinion to myself and said nothing as we brought him into the dining room and placed the box on two chairs we pushed together.

Marlaina was soothed that we were doing all we could for our new bunny friend, and got busy playing in her room while I vacuumed. As I cleaned, I plotted and played out all the ways I could sneak the poor creature outside and bury him without my daughter noticing.

I kept vacuuming and putting laundry away while I thought on my dilemma. I became so engrossed in my housework that I nearly forgot about the bunny until I passed through the dining room and the box loomed before me. I sadly approached, realizing I needed to stop procrastinating and handle the situation to the best of my ability.

No one was more surprised than me to find the rabbit simply GONE!!!!!

There was nothing in the box except the rumpled towel.

I was still processing this extraordinary happenstance when our dog Margaret came racing into the room, adding fuel to an inferno that I hadn't seen coming: we now had a rather large rabbit running around inside our home with a dog who would happily tear him to shreds.

Frantically, I raced from room to room, praying I wouldn't find Peter dead for the second time that day. The situation felt increasingly desperate. And the dog? Margaret was chasing after me like we were playing some new game and she was bound and determined to win herself a prize.

Margaret winning "the prize" was exactly what I was afraid of, too.

Suddenly I froze, listening. Was that a scratching sound coming from the corner of the living room by the piano? Yes, it was!

I grabbed the dog and dashed to my bedroom, putting her down and shutting the door to keep one of my problems safely contained. Then I snatched the bed spread from my bed and flew back downstairs, praying that Peter would still be in the living room where I'd last seen him.

Thank goodness, there he was! Peter froze in place, looking at me with terror in his eyes, while I angled in toward him, casting a wide net with the bedspread in hopes of capturing him.

Yes, I'd done it! Peter was trapped safely inside the blanket, and I couldn't believe that in mere moments this nightmare would be behind me.

I sprinted through the sunroom and out onto the deck, opening and spreading the blanket until Peter hopped off under a tree, nibbling grass and appearing none the worse for wear.

I stumbled back inside, overcome by all the stress and near-misses of the day, but full of joy for an unbelievably dramatic ending. And Marlaina? Well, she missed all the drama, but she swears to this day she never doubted that Mommy would make sure Peter Rabbit got home in time for dinner.

From sneaking her pet mice into her 5th grade classroom to creating a cozy winter home for the ladybugs she finds on her ceiling in the fall, **Linda Sherman-Kedersha** enjoys a special relationship with all creatures great and small.

Now retired after thirty plus years in the medical field, she is able to devote her time to introducing and sharing with her grandchildren the wonderful, magical world of bugs, birds, and bunnies, etc. It doesn't get much better than that!

TOAD
CROSSING
KOA

Froggy Went aFortin'

BY TAMIRA THAYNE

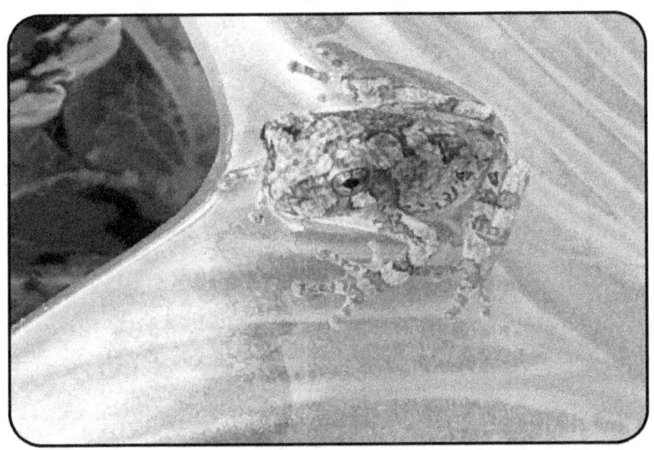

P^{lop.}

"What was that?" I wondered, just as something burst from the watering can I was filling and richocheted off my thumb.

Confused, I pulled my dreamy stare from the trees outside my kitchen window and turned my attention to the sink, where water still ran full tilt into the as-yet-unfull pail.

There—clinging to the rim of my blue watering can—sat a gray tree frog, blinking up at me as if to say, "WTH, lady! Why you messin' with my domicile?"

Fearing for his life, I lunged for him—with my hand since he's, you know, tiny—but the slippery fellow evaded my clutches and disappeared from sight.

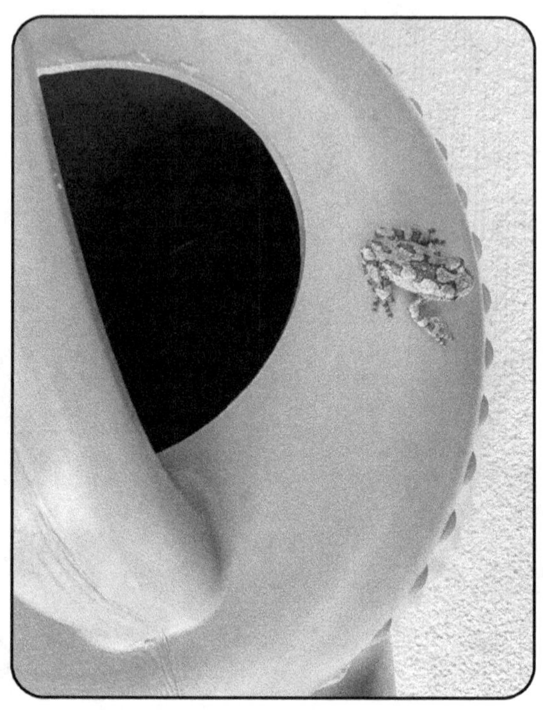

That's not good.

My mind raced to all the dangers that could befall an adorable little gray tree frog in my house.

Cats!

Garbage disposal!

My husband's clomping foot.

My own clomping foot.

Oh, the terror!

Time stopped, and I demanded Joe cease whatever obviously-less-important task he was doing at the stove and help me find Gray's Afrogamy—without moving, of course, due to the aforementioned foot-clomping.

First, I scoured the floor, repeatedly, because if nothing else I was newly cognizant of how wily tree frogs can be; plus, at the miniscule size of 1.5-2 inches in body length, the little guy could easily blend into our similarly-colored flooring and bore no chance of surviving a clomping.

Satisfied he wasn't on the floor and within reach of feet or claws, I turned my attention to my attire and my bare arms, giving myself a thorough once-over and having Joe check my back. Nope, no clingons—which left the sink or, worst case scenario, the garbage disposal.

My mind couldn't help but conjure up the ghastly horrors of disposal meets frog, and now you, my trusty readers, are likely picturing it, too. (You're welcome.)

I can hear you all now: "Hey! This is supposed to be a funny book. Ain't nuttin' funny about a frog in a disposal, ya' arschlock."

True, true. My bad. I blame my dastardly imagination, and invite you to do the same.

If there's one thing the hubs knows, it's that nothing sets his wife off like the threat of imminent death to a critter under her watch. He's more likely than not to jump into immediate action for his own self-preservation, a way to avoid all the wailing and mayhem that is sure to follow.

I tried to rein in my panic, understanding that the frenetic vibe I was putting off could make a helpless frog wish for death rather than the purgatory of finding oneself in a foreign land— never mind a garbage disposal, for Peta's sake.

The ghastly maw of said disposal mocked me, a clear frog-sized hole open and jonesing for its next victim.

"Release that frog this instant!" I challenged, raising my first in my best Braveheart impression. I was met only with silence.

"I said, unhand that frog," I insisted, carefully shining a flashlight into its murky depths and gingerly pushing the rubber tongues aside to scope out as much as I could before diving in.

While I fished for a frog in a place no fish or frog would deign to be, Joe busied himself at floor level, both to keep the cats away and in hopes that Mr. Afrogamy was wisely hiding himself elsewhere.

Joe's expedition proved fruitful, and even he—stalwart fellow that he is—released a whoop of hallelujah when he discovered Gray clinging to the underside of the sink cabinet.

Hooray! Froggy was alive, well, and could imminently return to his fortin' ways.

Joe swept the little fellow into his roomy palm and we hurried him outside to our bird bath in case he needed a good soak while pondering his next move. I felt his eyes ajudgin' me as I watered the nearby plants, and I was forced to defend myself vigorously while he responded only with a slow-blink froggy glare.

"How was I supposed to know you were in there?"

"It's my watering can, not yours, Gray's Afrogamy!"

"Fine, I'll allow that it's half yours, by virtue of possession (even by tiny critters) bein' 9/10 of the law 'round here. But I need to use it too, so we're gonna have to come up with some kind of arrangement for the future…deal?"

Gray treated the gray adirondack chairs like his own personal trees

I took his glare as a sign of acquiescence, and we spent the remainder of the summer in a shared joint custody agreement of said watering can. For my part, I ensured the gaping maw of the garbage disposal was suitably contained, and I always searched for the little frog before carrying the pail inside to fill at the sink.

Regardless, more often than not Gray's Afrogamy would appear from seemingly nowhere once the can began to fill, the telltale *plop* letting me know he'd dropped into the water and was about to fling himself up and over the edge.

But now I was ready and waiting for him…no more staring out the window for this girl, nosirree! I was in position, feet akimbo, hands up and poised to capture any adorable little frog who might burst from his watery prison and try his luck with my cats instead.

Not today, Gray!

I fell in love with the little guy over the summer, as I'd never before formed a relationship with a frog. Then Gray disappeared for a couple of weeks and I took it hard, even durn hard, fearing he'd rejected me and wandered off for bluer watering cans. *Or worse.*

I continued my nightly waterings, reminiscing about the good ole froggy days of yore.

Then one sunny day—much to my delight—the frogmeister himself reappeared, back from his walkabout and having learned a new trick: instead of "hanging out" along the insides of the can, he created a loft apartment for himself in the handle, and I only saw him when he deigned to appear for a chat.

I had been afraid to get too attached to Froggy Went aFortin', presuming I'd only have the one summer with the lad. But I recently read that Gray Tree Frogs can survive subzero temps, burying themselves beneath mulch or other substrates to get through the winter, and live for 7-9 years in the wild.

Well, that changes things! *You mean I might be able to spend multiple summers with my first froggy love?* Count me in.

Now I eagerly await the return of Gray's Afrogamy in the coming spring thaw, and have been checking my front porch daily for any signs of his Frogginess.

Nothing yet, but I've got my blue watering can all spruced up and ready…

THIS IS HOW
I USE THE
TREADMILL

Amazing Grace

BY MARTHA MOSLEY

My rescue dog was missing.

She had gotten away from her first adopter, too, so I guess I shouldn't have been surprised when it happened to us. A door had been inadvertently left open upon our return from the dog park, and the next thing I knew Grace was full-bore racing for the world beyond our driveway. This dog had lots of experience in running, and she put it to good use.

Grace's first adopter was an older man who thought an old dog would make a great companion. Grace probably was a fine companion for the few days that she stayed with him; however, the first chance she got she made a run for it. Posters, phone calls, and a lot of luck got her back, but he decided she was too much dog for him and returned her to the rescue.

The second adopter kept her secure but had other difficulties. It turns out Grace had no interest in learning house manners and relieved herself whenever and wherever she liked. The couple were not amused when their home became a doggie toilet.

Walking on a leash wasn't for Grace either; she would simply drop to the ground like a fat old stone and refuse to go anywhere. When they couldn't walk her or housebreak her, they decided she wasn't the dog for them.

I picked up this long-eared adoption-failure of a dog, intending only to keep her overnight until the rescue could take her back. When I realized she would use the doggie door and got along well with my other dogs, I figured that was a good indication she ought to stay here with us.

She was a canine anchovy, my Gracie. It was hard to get a taste for her, but once you did, you wanted more. . . . and that's how she ended up staying here with us, and why she was now running amok in my neighborhood.

I knew the rule about not chasing an escaping dog. Yet, when I saw her heading up the driveway, I'll be the first to admit I followed that rule for all of ten seconds. When she began to run faster, I ditched the rules and charged after that old dog like my feet were on fire.

From a distance, I watched her disappear into the underbrush. There is a lake behind our house, and woods, and innumerable places for a dog to hide. My husband and I searched them all, walking for miles. We called until our voices croaked and whistled until our lips cracked. Every time we heard a rustle or a creak, we were sure we had found her. We had not.

Exhausted, filthy, and defeated, we finally trudged home. On sore feet, I went to close the tailgate I'd left open when I came home from the park. I thought I simply imagined movement in the back of my car; I was so tired and stressed I was seeing things now…

But I wasn't!

There, indeed, was Grace, just hanging out in the car: clean, dry, and rested.

Our newest family member greeted me with joyful exuberance. "Where have you been? I thought you were lost."

My life with dogs has featured a bunch of tricks, surprises, and rude awakenings. Grace provided them all. She showed up in unexpected places doing zany things for all the days she was ours.

If there truly is a Rainbow Bridge, I'll know I've arrived because I'll hear that hound-y soprano's happy serenade.

"Where have you been? I thought you were lost."

Martha Mosley has spent a lifetime enjoying animals of all types and rescuing those who need it. Her children's book, **A Place for Grace,** is available on Amazon and recognizes the value of the seasoned love that older dogs offer. She also has had stories published in the *Chicken Soup for the Soul* series.

Martha lives in New Jersey with her husband Howard and adult offspring Michelle and Andrew. Their household has three dogs: Gigi a pit mix, Ella a border collie mix, and Sasha a dachshund.

She spends time reading, gardening, volunteering and walking their dogs.

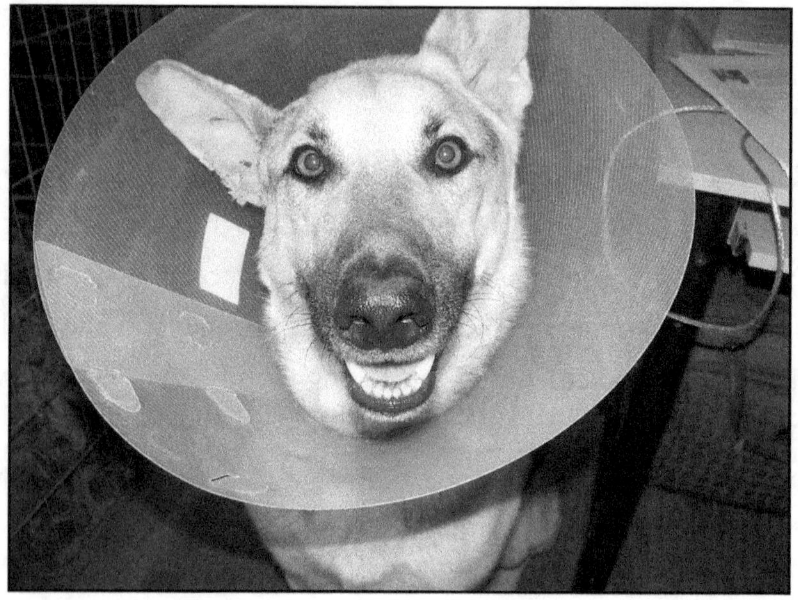

Does this cone make my teeth look whiter?

My Kingdom for a Chippy

BY TAMIRA THAYNE

I developed an obsession with chipmunks and bunnies because the Virginia woods where we lived had been overhunted by larger predator animals. What you don't see every day turns into the equivalent of a unicorn sporting faery lights, I suppose.

So anytime I spotted these seemingly common animals, my eyes would light with excitement and I'd fall all over myself to spend time in their general vicinity.

We'd barely arrived at our campsite in Littleton, Massachusetts, when I beheld Unicorn #1, in the form of a little chippy we'd be sharing our lives with for the next week.

"Yippee!" I shouted in my head, noting Joe's lack of enthusiasm for our tiny, rodenty lot mate. I, for one, adored that

we were nestled into a wooded locale surrounded by tall trees and small chipmunk homes. What could be better?

I discovered "our" chippy made his home right near a rock by the septic line. *OK, maybe he wasn't the wisest of chippies—or maybe he "won" that craptastic locale in a booby prize contest—*but he was still here and I'd get to interact with him every day, which was all that mattered!

I immediately set about plotting how to introduce myself, what kind of treats I could offer a chipmunk, and pondering the eternal question of whether he would be my Valentine or not. That last desire made me particularly nervous, because putting myself on the line like that also left me wide open for the worst possible outcome: chippy rejection.

Full disclosure, I didn't know if "he" was really a dude chipmunk or not [there was a vibe], but I'm an equal opportunity chippy snuggler anyway, so I was all in regardless.

On Day One I procured [yes, these are for ME, honey], some shelled sunflower seeds and created a little pile in sight of my camper window. Within moments, Linus (come on, that's the perfect chippy name) was onsite fillin' up.

How did he get there so fast? Super smell, super sight? Maybe I should investigate, or you can just educate me instead, which sounds easier now that I think about it.

I dug out my camera with the long lens so I could get up close and personal without getting up close and personal, then I stacked seeds around the campsite so I could watch him discover the next and the next and then carry his booty off to his lair.

As I watched I fell deeper in lurve with his chubby cheeks, and unsolicited baby talk came splurting outta my mouth. "Oooh, come to momma, little guy! I just wanna kiss those ample cheekies, please?"

I rushed toward him (no, I didn't), arms reaching and pleading for his paw in the most demeaning fashion possible, while he gave me the side-eye and slipped through the cutouts of the fireplace in which I'd attempted to entrap him.

He, because he was an upstanding chipmunk and probably didn't swear—even to himself—replied, "Good seeds, Nutto, but you're not getting those freaky lips anywhere near THESE cheekies. Now that I've filled my coffers, kindly remove your nasty poo-mobile from my proppity before I call the animal popo."

But because I didn't speak Chippish (which will be rectified when Duolingo gets onboard), I ignored his little outburst and continued my attempts to woo his chipmunk heart until the day we rambled off to greener woodlands.

I left him a big pile of seeds to show there were no hard feelings despite the continued sting of his rejection. Heck, maybe someday he'll show up on my doorstep with some little violets and a seed or two of his own to win back my heart.

A girl can dream.

UNLESS YOUR DOG
CAN DO THIS...
Please
Be Responsible and
Clean Up After Them!
Thank you!

DOG
LIBRARY
TAKE A
STICK
LEAVE A
STICK

Couching It:
Tips from the Beagle

BY **C**HRISTY **B**URBIDGE

Hi, I'm Sophie, writing you from the Rainbow Bridge where I've spent the past several years playing and hanging out with newfound friends. I say "several" years, because what's a year to a dog, anyway? As the saying goes, "time is nonlinear"—much like the way I walk when I'm feeling tired or particularly lazy.

I came to live with my family in the spring of 2009, when Facebook was in its prime. *(More on this later.)* I'm told I was born on a farm on the bucolic island of Martha's Vineyard, the runt of a litter of angelic bluetick beagles. I'm unaware of the details, but who remembers the specifics of their birth anyway?

No one, that's who.

What I do remember is that on a cloudless Sunday morning in May of that year, an older couple scooped me up and promised they'd find me a home through a shelter program in Middletown, Rhode Island. That sounded good to me, so we boarded a cab with their beagle and made our way to the ferry.

A fun fact about the cab system in Martha's Vineyard in those days, which I'll refer to as "ancient times": most of the cabs were called "rideshares," which meant that different people would hop in and out at sundry points along the same journey.

Many people complained about these rideshares—because they forced you to cram in with strangers—but I never understood this myself. In my world, that's just more people for me to love, and, most importantly, more people to adore me!

Where was I…Oh, yeah. So we were on our way to the ferry that day, and we stopped to pick up another couple who was also headed for the ferry. These two women boarded the cab and made tedious small talk with my rescuers, as people tend to do.

"Would you like a puppy?" asked the Rescue Lady half in jest, picking me up and showing me off.

"We wish," replied the second couple in unison, laughing and elbowing one another. "Jinx!"

One of them continued, "While we both love dogs, we've never had one and wouldn't know the first thing about caring for the little guy. Besides, we're staying with my parents until our house is finished. They really aren't 'dog people.'"

What does that even mean, I wondered, that her parents "weren't dog people?" That's like saying, "I'm not an air person," or "I'm not really keen on drinking fluids." Is there even an option to be anything else?

No. No there isn't.

"Okay," shrugged the woman from the animal rescue. "It was worth a shot. If you change your mind before the end of the ferry ride," she continued, "let us know."

Later, just as the ferry was about to dock, a middle-aged Kardashian-looking woman—wearing a fur coat of all things— emerged out of nowhere and approached me. "What a cute little beagle baby! I'll take her if you're still looking for a home?"

Now, we've all heard stories about the power of a dog's sense of smell, except I can assure you there is no word in the English language to describe the magnitude of this woman's perfume. It was downright painful to my sensitive olfactory nerves, I will tell you that much.

Zoinks! I was still a puppy and didn't know everything, but I knew I didn't want to go home with "Dogatella Versace." *Not today, not ever!*

It was then that the new couple from the cab stepped up to the plate, and I remember feeling surprised because I hadn't even known they fancied me. *Who could blame them, though?*

"Actually, we've just decided to adopt her ourselves," one of the women from the couple said, a sense of urgency in her voice.

"Well," pouted the Kardashian wannabe, "if you change your mind, here's my number."

I watched my new moms grimace as they took her number, and I'm fairly certain I destroyed that little scrap of paper later. I mean, I was a puppy after all, so it probably had nothing to do with the fact that I didn't want her anywhere near me, right?

I do know that I slept like the baby I was on the ride to my new home, waking only for a stop at the local pet store where we bought my first bed, blanket, and toys.

Time flew by, and my moms and I—along with my brother Paulie—built an amazing life together, although it goes without saying that I had a lot of training to do with them.

You know, dog newbies and all.

Before I landed at the Rainbow Bridge after a battle with lymphoma, I let my moms build me my own Facebook page, which was a delightful tool to feature my antics and highlight the world of animal rescue. Below, I flaunt some of my most share-worthy posts for your perusal.

The couch "before" and "after"

Since the title of this book involves couches and dogs,

naturally I'm obligated to start by showing off THIS particular post.

I wish I could take full credit for this couch accomplishment, but my brother Paulie worked harder than me and was able to make the "final push through."

Now that you understand how seriously I take my doggie duties, let's look at a few particularly helpful posts and analyze what worked well and what I might have done differently. After that I will offer some tips for humans, in case any of my readers are considering building your furry family member into a social media star.

July 17:

That awkward moment when you're eating someone's lawn, and you can FEEL the person looking out their window, shaking their head . . . and you can FEEL the embarrassment of your walking companions, who are anxiously begging you to move along and mind your own business. But, but, but . . . you just can't stop!*

**The comments I received on this post were uncommonly supportive. Reaching out to others in your moments of weakness and receiving unexpected compassion? It's definitely one of life's greatest blessings. Try it sometime.*

July 27:

It was absolutely my privilege to rise at 5:00 am to lead the neighborhood pack in a rousing song. I trust it was enjoyed by all.*

It's important to showcase your strengths, but at the same time, give a nod to those who have helped you get to where you are. Here I fell short by neglecting to list the names of my canine comrades who helped me successfully wake an entire neighborhood on a Sunday morning. I know, not cool...

August 1:

This machine is "ocupado" right now. Why don't you go ahead and get started on the bike, then come back in 20 minutes or so?*

Years ago, I threw up on the belt of this treadmill. When vomiting on a treadmill, the belt is the most ideal part to aim for. The subsequent stain, set to spin round and round for all eternity, will serve as a reminder of your presence forever. You know, in case your moms ever try to forget you!

August 22:

Tonight I have the opportunity to see a fireworks show. While the thought of eating sticky wrappers off the ground and being touched by a mass of strangers thrills me to pieces, the noise may be too much for me. I'll have to play this one by ear.*

This post garnered a hearty number of "likes," but it gets awfully close to a truth I don't advertise: I'm attracted to creepy people! For example, we used to attend a Sunday playgroup at the pet store, but I always gravitated away from the other dogs and toward the most sinister-looking humans. I've come to understand this is not information others care to know about me. While I appreciated the volume of "likes," I can't help but wonder if some of them were "pity likes." Hey, any like is probably a good like, though, right?

August 25:

No, I did NOT rip the strap off a pedal on the exercise bike. The exercise bike must have done that all by itself! It's sad how some people—and things—can't take responsibility for their actions.*

It was wrong of me to call the strap out on a public forum. I would NOT recommend doing this. Later that day, he and I ended up exchanging harsh words between ourselves.

August 29:

Sometimes when you call my name, all I can do is stare at you blankly. It's like I don't even know you....*

As true as this is, in retrospect, I don't know if I should have shared it. This post came off as rude, but I wasn't trying to be. It's just that I simply don't care to listen to certain people on days ending with a "y."

Helping your animal build a social media career: tips for humans

These will be my last words of wisdom to you, so pay attention, folks:

1. Adopt, for f---'s sake. This should be common sense, people! And I know I just said a bad word, and "good little beagle girls don't swear." I blame it on my premature exposure to the Internet, personally. After all, if I weren't rescued, I wouldn't have built the social media platform that I did, and I wouldn't have been exposed to all those bad words that are so fun to say!

2. Keep in mind the ultimate goal: to help others. After my passing, my parents got involved with various canine lymphoma research foundations. My Facebook page served as the springboard for this, so it's not all just fun and games. We're doing life-changing work!

3. Ignore the haters. This is important no matter the circumstances. There are always going to be neigh-sayers. Regardless, you've got to put your best paw forward and do what's best for everyone involved, including YOU.

4. Be prepared to meet people you otherwise wouldn't have. The seeds of some best friendships have been sown on Facebook only to eventually bloom in person.

For example, I once went to a pool party and met one of my moms' work colleagues in person for the first time. When I approached her and felt inspired to hump her leg, we both felt like we already "knew" one another.

She let me hump away to my heart's content, when otherwise she might have been less tolerant of what could only be described as "my friendly overture."

5. Have fun! Life is short.
No one knows this better than I.

If I can leave you with one last tip, it's this: Don't wait to be invited onto the couch. Whatever it is you want in life, go for it. *You got this!*

Christy Burbidge is the author of four children's books: *Paulie the Piping Plover's Merry Misfits: A Martha's Vineyard Tale*, *Paulie the Piping Plover's Sea Turtle Rescue*, *Claire's Coyote Friends*, and *If Memory Surfs: A Book for Healing*.

Her recent flash fiction and other works have appeared in *Akitsu Quarterly*, *Otherwise Engaged: Literature and Arts Journal*, and *Ruff Drafts*. Since 2022, she has served as a judge for the annual Dog Writers Association of America competition.

Christy lives outside of Boston with her spouse and two rescue beagles.

My Kingdom
A Book
And Thee

The New York Stork
Brings My Kind of Babies

BY TAMIRA THAYNE

I love most critters, from afar at least. And while I strive to be an equal opportunity critter admirer, a loosely-guarded secret of mine is that cats are my all-time fav. *I can't help it!*

As early as I can remember I was dragging cats around with me, apparently even preferring them to my Easter basket and, gasp, **chocolate.** I love how soft their pelts feel, and I most adore snuggling up in their oh-so-delicious fur. It's my favorite form of therapy.

Me holding a cat beside my Easter basket, my brothers to my left.

As such I'd both looked forward to meeting cats on the road and dreaded it, because if they were in dire straits I knew I would be forced to take action on their behalf. *Which sounded like a lot of emotional pain.*

Plus, if the cats are the "property" of another, the situation can and often does end badly; these folks are seldom interested in help or outside opinions.

For some inexplicable reason, and to my heart's detriment, we found ourselves spending a month in New York state, which included three weeks at a campground outside of Malone near the Canadian border.

Here, as fortune would have it, lived three striped brother cats. These boys "belonged" to the owners of the campground. They were not neutered.

And they seemed hungry.

I know, I know, to my mind's eye every animal looks like he or she could eat a water buffalo. (Apologies to bison the world over.) But these cats were stahving dahling, I swear to you. You're just gonna have to trust me on that.

However—being cats—they made ends meet the best they could by wisely working the campground crowd for their fill of snacks and snuggles.

It didn't take long for them to identify their latest soft touch, me, who scrambled to serve them a heaping bowl of yum anytime they made their way to my doorstep.

The most gregarious of the three was a boy I dubbed "Finally," because I was FINALLY in some kitty-lovin' heaven. Once he marked me as his primary food source I saw him every day without fail, and was rewarded many times over with purrs and snuggles when his tank was topped off and he was feeling a bit nappy.

It wasn't long before his shyer brother joined us (all stripes, no white), but I didn't meet the third and final brother until we were readying for departure. By this point I was totally in love with Finally and Furrily, and worried about them getting enough to eat when I was gone.

Did the owners expect them to hunt for their food? Would they provide more nourishment when all the campers were gone? Would they get them the vet care they needed, neuter them? I didn't know, but I vowed to speak to the owner about it on our way out.

That morning I prepped two big bowls of food and fretted when the boys were no-shows. I tucked the offerings behind a tree so the cats could find them but they wouldn't be so quickly visible (and tossed!) by campground staff.

Then I spotted the by-now-familiar stripes and white paws stopping by for a bite and raced over to greet my baby. *Finally! But wait…there was no white stripe on his nose!* Here indeed was the elusive third brother.

"Frenzily" ravenously gobbled both bowls of chow, so I quickly refilled them before I left in hopes that all three brothers could enjoy one more meal on me.

Now I think of them often and speculate that I got a mite too attached. The owner of the campground assured me the cats were well-loved family members, but I still harbored doubts.

As much as I enjoyed greeting those handsome lads each morning and providing them with snacks and sustenance, I postulate that I'm better off NOT meeting any more campground cats.

I get plum overwhelmed what with all the fretting.

Remember, happy thoughts, Tami. Happy thoughts.

J Like Snow.
Really.

Buddy the GoPro Star

BY JOSEPH HORVATH

Our dog Buddy, a Heinz-57 mix of husky, lab, pit, chow chow, and shepherd, was an avid explorer of the 35 wooded acres we owned in rural Virginia. Unfortunately for us, more often than not he managed to find some foul-smelling "something" to roll around in, necessitating a bath.

I decided to find out where he was locating these putrid substances, so I bought a dog chest harness for my GoPro and attached it to Buddy. I then sent him on his way with high expectations of some great video footage and finally some insight into his travels around the property.

One thing I always did when I recorded was look at the camera to make sure that the little red light was on since I'm not the most trustful person when it comes to technology . . . or people for that matter.

Thirty minutes later Buddy was back, sans GoPro and sans chest harness; he was just a stinky dog with a somewhat-satisfied smirk on his face. I knew the camera had been running when I released him to explore, so the recording still had awhile to go before the battery officially died.

My wife Tami and I walked the property immediately, and then on and off for a couple of weeks looking for the GoPro to no avail. It was missing and presumed dead.

While I'd been outmaneuvered by the dog this time, I had the brilliant idea to buy another chest harness and a used GoPro and try the experiment again. Fool me once and all that.

This time I was on top of it, though, and attached long yellow "caution" streamers to the harness and a Tile geo tag to the GoPro. I attached the GoPro to the harness and the harness to Buddy and very smugly sent Buddy off again to do his worst.

Twenty minutes later he returned, again with no GoPro and no harness. That feeling of deja vu hit hard.

I jumped on the quad and began driving the property looking for the harness, hoping it would be easy enough to spot with the addition of the streamers. After about 30 minutes, I found the harness by the river, but the GoPro was no longer attached.

I could't figure how he got the GoPro out of the harness since it snapped in. I was also perplexed as to how he removed a harness that went over his head and connected behind his front legs.

I assumed the GoPro landed in the river somewhere, never to be seen again. To be sure, though, since it was geotagged, I got my phone and started driving around with the Tile app open just in case. It took about an hour of circling and then finally crawling on my hands and knees through the brush before I found the second GoPro.

The camera had enough memory to record two hours of video. When I watched the recording, it featured exactly two minutes of Buddy running and one hour and 58 minutes of the sky. The crazy dog had raced straight to a fallen tree not far from the house, brushed under the tree, and knocked the camera off. The camera landed with the lens facing upwards and filmed the clouds until the memory card was full.

If you thought that was the end of the story you would be mistaken, since I sent TWO cameras out and only recovered one. Fast forward six months and we're into the new year. Spring is in the air and Buddy has found himself a girlfriend in the form of a yellow labrador retriever who lived only ¼ mile from us through the woods.

That girl was trouble from the get-go, though, and had already earned him the name "Colonel Sanders" from the county animal jail guards. But that's a different story.

His girlfriend, let's call her Lola, had escaped her yard again and her family drove over to our house looking for her. I wasn't there, but Tami was home when they arrived. During the course of the conversation, they asked if we had lost a GoPro camera the year prior.

Tami was shocked by the segue and exclaimed, "Yes, as a matter of fact we did! Why, did you happen to find it?"

It turned out that the year before when I looked at the camera to ensure it was recording, I was standing in front of our house. Lola's owners had found our camera on their property and watched the video to see if they could figure out who it belonged to. When they arrived at our home in their search for Lola, they recognized our house from the video.

Tami called to tell me that the camera had been found, and I would need to drive over to the neighbors' when I got home to retrieve it. "Yes!" I thought. "Finally, all the mysteries of Buddy's wanderings will be revealed."

Alas, there was nothing more exciting in this footage than the last. It seemed that Buddy was a bit of a wanderer and tended to boldly ignore property lines. The camera sported ten minutes of Buddy running through the woods, but no clues as to how he managed to dump the camera and harness before he got down to the important task of finding something gross to roll in.

I learned my lesson after the second GoPro and never sent another camera out with Buddy.

Turns out it was a lot of effort with an equal share of disappointment; and, whether by accident or some unique (and marketable!) skill, the dog was adept, too adept, at removing the harness and camera to get down to the business of his dirty work.

Buddy two, Joe zero.

As a child of Hungarian immigrants, **Joseph Horvath** is a first-generation American who grew up in Pennsylvania and was immersed in the Hungarian culture until he joined the U.S. Air Force at the age of 18. He became a cryptologic linguist and later an imagery analyst until his retirement from the military.

Joseph is father to identical twin sons and became a grandfather in 2025. He holds a Master's degree in Geographic Information Systems and a Master's in Organizational Management. He continued his career supporting the U.S. Government for another 24 years before his final retirement in 2026.

Joseph enjoys hiking and traveling and has been to all 50 states and over 30 countries.

Are these even my kids?

Owl's Way
Who's Gonna Tell Him?

The Possum Wrangler(s)

BY TAMIRA THAYNE

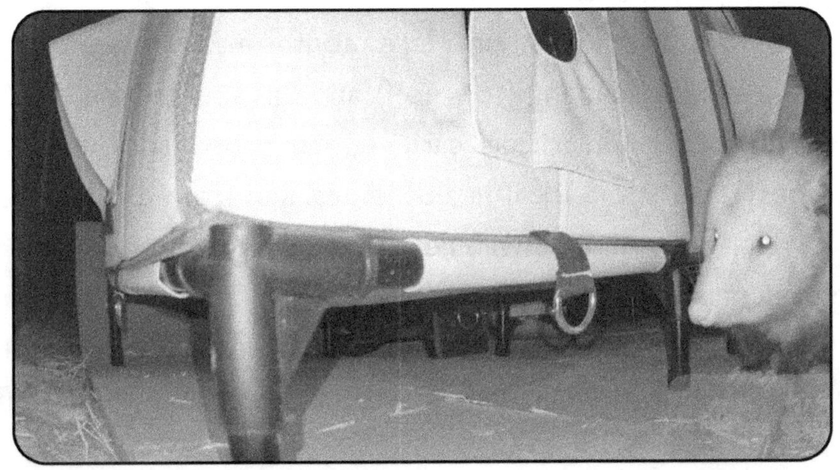

I shouldna' done it. I know that now.

But I did. I complained about the 'possum, (henceforth shortened to possum) and then a whole lotta calamity—in the form of an errant husband—came a'callin for me.

Or for Krimp, actually.

When we moved to our West Virginia home, I was the teensiest bit lonely. Not for people, of course, but for animals, because animals are my happy place.

New home, cue new happy place auditions in three, two, one…

I needed to get some animals into my world, stat! We'd just survived a northern Virginia Extended Stay hotel for five months while our house was being built, a pretty small cage for two adults and a sick kitty. By the time our home was move-in ready, I was jonesing for an eyeful of ANY wildlife…squirrel, skunk, bear, you name it, I wanted—no, needed—to see it.

But we now resided in a—*gasp*—subdivision, and even though this offered me low hopes of befriending critters beyond my own back door, I was determined to try.

I would soon get my wish. Mere months into our residency, I spotted a fox with mange (oh, no!!), and this spurred me to take my neighborhood critter care duties more seriously; we obviously had some local health issues, and from experience I knew that government wildlife agencies most-often refuse to help animals in need.

Sometimes Ma and Pa Kettle in their rural homes are all the animals have in their corner; if we care we have to educate ourselves on how we can best provide aid.

By December I'd installed two heated cat houses under our back deck for local strays to warm up in the frigid winter temps, as well as a heated water bowl and some basic food stations.

I assumed the houses would be inhabited by cats since I'd identified at least four of the roaming variety, but soon Krimp— one of my possum friends who remains blithely unaware of our budding relationship—decided to "hang out" behind the cat houses, moseying for hours between the water, food, and his restin' and bathing spot, crunching kibble as he went.

As an equal opportunity critter voyeur I was cool with it, except for the part where Krimp took up residence directly in front of the cathouse critter cam, setting it off every 30 seconds from here to infinity and beyond.

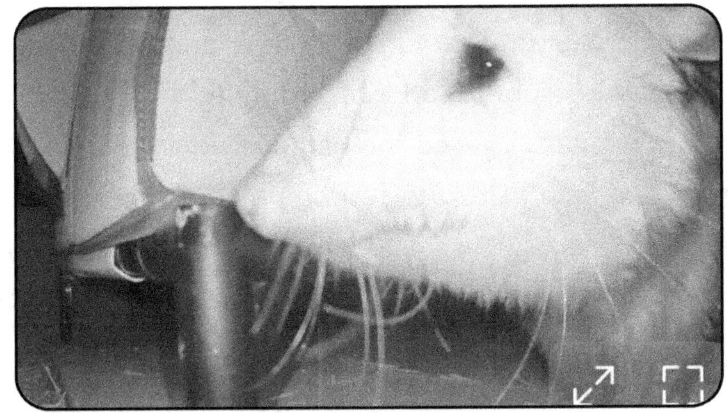

I was visiting my daughter in her home near Philadelphia, Pennsylvania, and noticed the camera alerts were coming in hawt and heavy. "What now?" I thought, jumping onto the camera app to creep on my backyard visitors as I tend to do morning, noon, and noche anyway.

Oh yep, there he was: it was the possum, Krimp, so-named because the back of his tail kinks to the left.

Krimp was sending me videos.

Every 30 seconds.

"Krimp," I begged through the 200-mile ether between us. "It's 10 degrees out there, even worse with the windchill. Please go INSIDE the cat house and make me the happiest animal lady in the sac (the cul-de-sac, that is). You know you wanna…it's FREEZING."

The boy went so far as to stick his nose and two front paws across the threshold of the house, but then he chickened out, dropping back onto the straw-covered ground.

Possums are highly susceptible to frostbite on their exposed ears, toes, and tail, so I knew he'd be safer and I could legit brag about my new possum friend if he would **JUST GO INSIDE.**

And that's what triggered the bad decision.

I complained about Krimp setting off the cameras.

To Joe.

Who is a man, and as a man he may have felt a certain compulsion to SOLVE HIS WIFE'S PROBLEM.

Which, again, to a man, most often means he must VANQUISH HER FOE using whatever methods he considers prudent.

Therefore, to Joe's way of thinking, Krimp the possum HAD TO BE REMOVED from the camera's view forthwith, henceforth, and forevermore. *Amen.*

Without consulting his wife, me, as to the efficacy of this bold move, my champion armed himself with a flashlight and broom, sallying forth to do battle with the innocuous Krimp; nevermind that said possum was simply trying to grab a couple winks back behind "the shed," and had no inkling of the strife headed his way.

Please remember that Joe was incredibly valiant, ok? Indeedy he was. That man gave it everything he had, separating those cat houses like he was Moses partin' the Red Sea. He probably even pulled off the arm flourish.

Krimp was beside himself at the invasion, hissing as the house's metal legs scraped across the tiles in front of him. "How dare you, intrepid fool! What is the meaning of this abuse of my possumhood?"

My warrior was all grit, however, and simply ignored the smaller being shrieking in his general direction. This could have been due to the fact that Joe doesn't speak possum or even critter, but for argument's sake we'll go with "he was unflappably brave" instead.

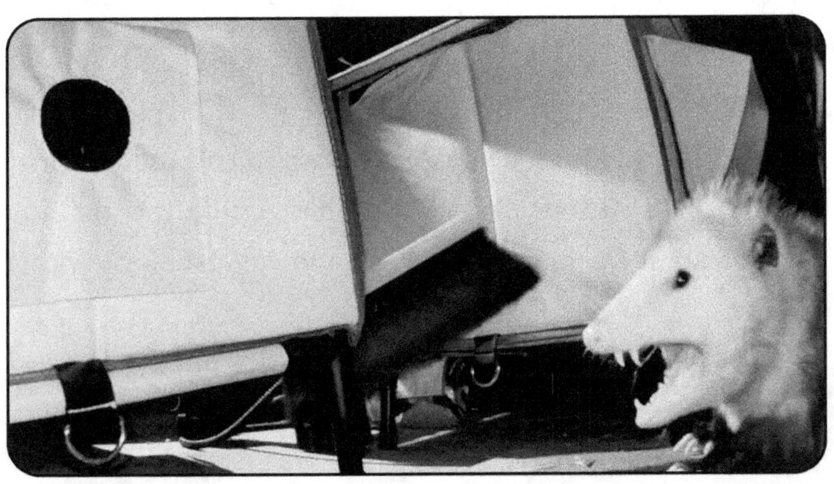

Krimp even bared his teeth at the usurper, making sure the crazy freak knew exactly what he was fixin' to get himself messed up in. "Look at these things! Fangs! Don't let the sweet disposition fool you, buddy. I'm bringin' receipts."

But "buddy" kept comin' after the tiny marsupial, a wide broom head with brown bristles bearing down on him and attempting to shoo him away from the camera.

Krimp stomped his foot, refusing to budge. "No, stoogecanoe! I'm staying right here, so you can forget about it, unless you want a piece of all this?"

Joe had clearly misjudged the will of his opponent, that much was obvious, but at least he knew when he was beat. He sighed, picked up his broom, and proceeded to—wisely—use it to knock over the camera instead.

Problem solved, for the time being at least.

The next night Krimp was back in "his" spot, and I was stressed about him freezing his freaky yoyo-ing nads off (google it!) and wishing he'd just **GO IN THE CRITTER HOUSE ALREADY.**

I told Joe, "You know, if you really wanted to vanquish my foe, you could pick Krimp up and push him inside the cat house, which would solve both my stress and his problem with the cold."

Joe was gobsmacked, even horror-struck. *"Say what now?"*

The Second Possum Wrangler

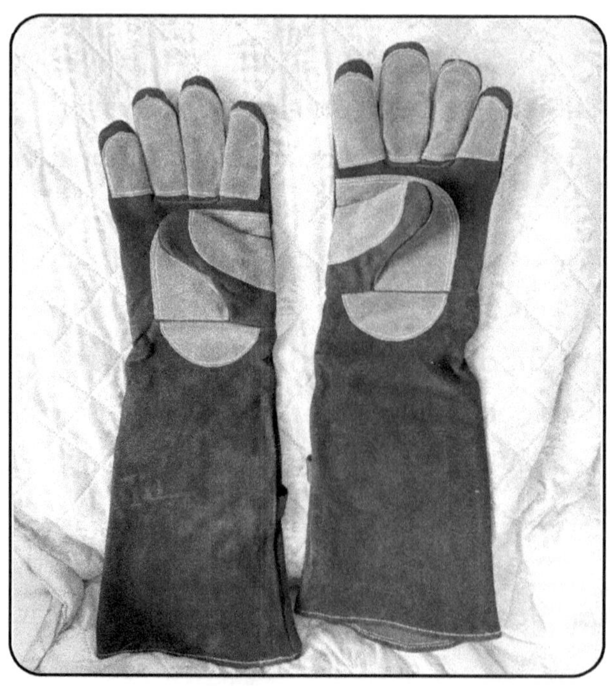

Even before I got home, I ordered myself a pair of possum wrangling gloves and hatched a plan to take matters into my own hands. The next cold snap I was gonna' get that possum into the warmth of a cat house one way or t'other.

My gloves arrived along with a second possum who promptly rendered them useless. Mensa earned her name when she bopped into the closest cathouse like she'd been doing it her whole life—all while Krimp still bumbled around outside. No one was more stunned than I!

When Krimp lumbered around the corner and spotted Mensa in the shelter he'd dreamed of accessing for days, he blustered with the best of his fellow menfolk. *"How DARE you, little girlie? Don't you know this is MY HOUSE."*

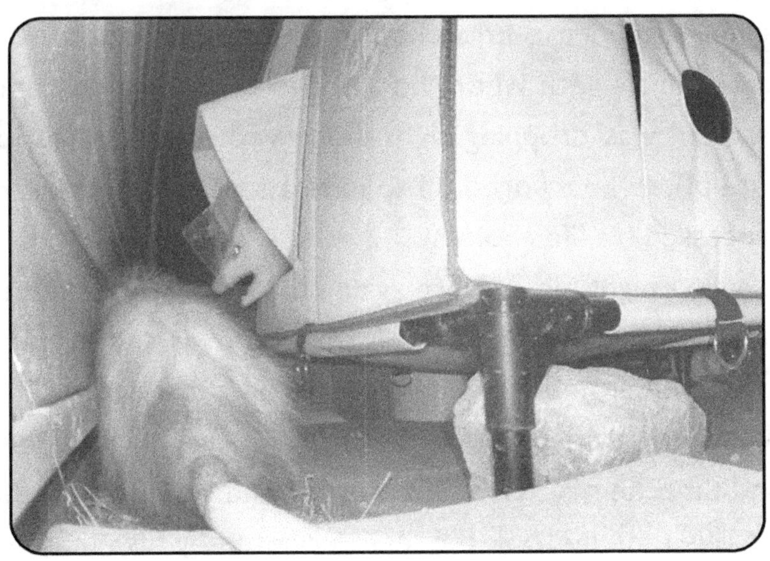

But Mensa, as an emancipated lady possum, was having none of it, and gave the burly fella a piece of her mind. "Pffft, please.

Have you even stepped foot into this hella warm den yet? No, no you haven't. First come first served, looooossseeeerrrr."

Krimp had been outmatched in the smarts department by the cute female with whom he'd hoped to share a den, and his self-esteem was dropping right along with his balls (seriously, look it up!), so he trudged off to have a snack and a drink while he processed his life choices.

The next night Mensa once again beat Krimp to the house he had claimed, and words in the form of growls and even some lunges were flung about as he tried his best to evict her.

When he failed to oust Mensa from "his" shelter for the second time, he realized all his plotting had been for naught.

But this time he took the lesson offered by his nemesis and put it to good use: he grumbled his way over to the house next door and pulled himself inside, leaving only the end of his tail dangling outside the door as a signal to other interested usurpers that it was indeed "ocupado."

He'd done it, all by himself! Well, with the help of a woman, but still…

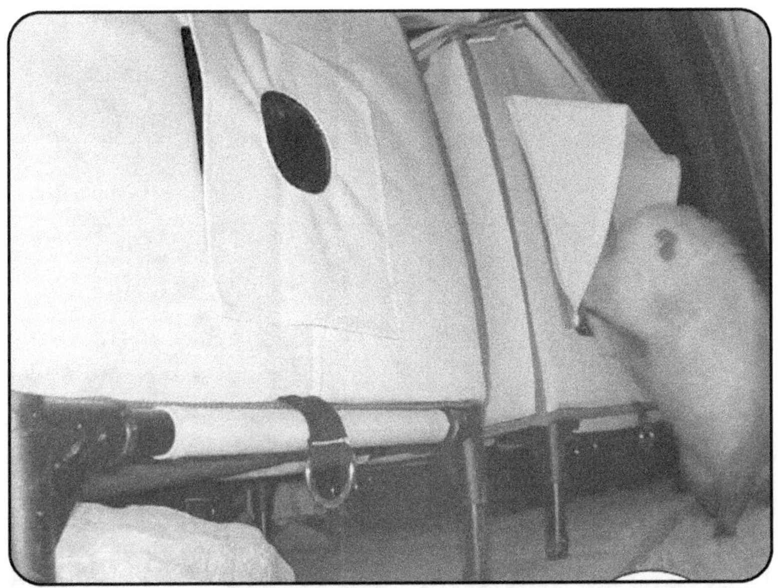

Krimp stayed in his warm den for hours that night and booked reservations for most subsequent cold weather bursts, too.

In the end, thanks to Mensa and his own perseverance, Krimp had rendered further wrangling unnecessary, but I didn't mind.

I'm sure that in my animal-crazed world those gloves will come in handy another time and in another place.

I probably don't look forward to it.

Possums leave footprints on your heart...in addition to your outside critter domiciles.

Guchguch: A Cancer Survivor's Antics

BY KUHU ROY

In India, stray dogs form an integral part of the fabric of a community. They play multiple roles—they are brilliant watchdogs, offer unparalleled loyalty and selfless love, and are guardians of elders and children alike, while their own life remains at constant peril.

My mother and I consider ourselves very fortunate to have cared for hundreds of stray dogs in Baroda, Gujarat, India over the past two decades. A desire to give back to society to ensure the public health and the plight of stray dogs in our city propelled us to serve man's best friend. At any given point, some three hundred stray dogs are under our care at different locations and are looked after for their entire lifetime. In addition to the daily feedings undertaken by my mother (seven hours of effort!), we ensure sterilization and vaccination against rabies—key elements for a mutually peaceful co-existence with mankind—as well as manage their medical needs and provide them a dignified farewell when their time comes.

We also give them all a name based on their unique personalities, since they all have an identity of their own and a massive zest for life despite the hardships that come their way. When they age and survival on the streets is no longer tenable, they come home to me. In two decades, fifty such precious souls have had a second chance at life by coming to live with us.

Unfortunately, many in India consider only puppies as adoptable. Since senior stray dogs, blind stray dogs, paralyzed stray dogs, and amputee stray dogs do not fit into the cuteness bracket, they are completely marginalized. Hence why our home has always welcomed these souls, and we marvel as their personalities flourish with the extra time, attention, and safety.

One such dog who came to light up our home with his antics we called Guchguch. Guchguch walked into my life in 2005 when I had just entered college. He was barely a couple of months old when his mother, Goshi (who lived on the college premises), showed up with him and seven other siblings. He was a plump pup, sporting long white fur with the occasional accent strands of fawn. Unlike his mischievous siblings, Guchguch was more the philosopher type, who stared at the trees in the college garden and seldom played despite their attempts to engage him.

Guchguch was particularly close to my mother, who met and fed him every morning during her daily rounds. In fact, thanks to Maa, my college premises remained a zero-rabies zone for twelve years—with zero stray dog multiplication—due to the sterilization and vaccination program we'd implemented. *We were over the moon!* Maa, as any doting grandmother would, often pampered and spoiled Guchguch with extra helpings of food, followed by a petting session.

Guchguch and I usually met in the evening. After a tiring day at college, his smiling face and glittering eyes never failed to bring me a sense of peace. We would sit together in the garden and he'd amuse me with somersaults, and then we followed up with snack time. If I saw Guchguch in the morning hours on my way to class, he would jump all over me, twisting and turning in joy, and I would walk into the classroom with muddy, paw-printed clothes. I confess there were days, in order to avoid the onslaught and subsequent "muddying," I entered the college grounds lurking behind bushes and shrubs.

Guchguch had a busy life all his own. His nails were completely rounded at the tips, a giveaway that he tended toward long jaunts to who-knows-where. He was often spotted at roadside food joints enjoying spicy meals with those who knew him and his spirit. In his spare time, he loved to take bullying digs at his sisters Tuki and Jukjuk, his only siblings to survive, who had become faithful subordinates to him. He often put them in their place, but never harmed them.

Jukjuk would pee in submission in acknowledgment of his superiority, averting her eyes and face from his stare. Despite the bullying, Jukjuk loved her brother to the moon and back, and followed him faithfully no matter what. We came to believe that Jukjuk looked forward to the daily torment from her brother, like an appetizer before dinnertime.

Guchguch enjoyed his routines for eleven years, but one day we noticed he was bleeding from the genital area. We rushed him to the vet, where it turned out he had a tumor. Surgery was the only way out. The vet felt the odds were in his favor, so we made the decision to move forward. Guchguch was rescued and brought into our home at last. The following morning, we flew a veterinary surgeon to our local area, and hours later we learned the surgery had been a success.

Guchguch was discharged and brought home.

Butter was a spoiled pup who'd been raised like a princess; she ruled our home. At the onset, she was angry with Guchguch's presence in her "domain." She growled and barked at Guchguch, showing no signs of relenting. Butter had been merely two months old when a car hit her, causing her injuries that needed daily support, and caring for her soon became a labor of love for both my mother and myself. She'd wormed her way into our hearts and lives!

By late afternoon, Butter's growls and barks transformed into concern for Guchguch instead of anger at him. She stepped inside his room and licked his forehead, then looked at me with grave concern in her eyes. I've learned to trust a dog's instinct. If not for Butter's timely warning convincing us to rush Guchguch to the vet, he probably would not have survived the post-surgery complication.

As Guchguch began to recover from the ordeal, I resumed my schedule—my doctoral dissertation was due for submission. One day when I returned home, my pillow was on the floor with all the cotton pulled out of it. "Did this pillow explode on its own?" I asked the innocently-posturing Guchguch, who lay proud as punch beside the torn pillow.

The following day, the replaced pillow met the same fate, again to an "I-don't-know-how-it-happened" expression on Guchguch's face. However, we would soon come to understand that these little displays were a mere curtain-raiser performance. What followed the next day left me shocked—and amused, I must confess. I returned home and opened the door to find Guchguch smiling, his eyes glittering with joy, standing over the unfortunate remains of my mattress.

He jumped around on the tattered bed, mighty delighted and barking, "Look what I made for you, Maa!" I imagined he'd say to me if he could.

I took him into a tight embrace and told him, "Guchguch, I have had the honor of saving scores of lives but believe me, I have never sought a reward. Your art creation is simply too beautiful for words!" He trotted off, happy with himself for a job well-done, but I did not know where to begin in clearing up the mess. I slept that night on the thorny remains of my mattress, coir pricking me every time I rolled over.

Knowing the fate pillows and mattresses of the house were now subjected to—and as a disaster management measure— Maa put a sign on her bedroom door: "No Guchguch allowed in this room!" We laughed then and still laugh about it now...

The mattress-tearing episode boosted Guchguch's confidence but enraged Butter, who liked discipline and order in her home. Guchguch approached Butter with the bullying style that had worked with his sisters, but he got beaten up by Butter on two different occasions, which left him bewildered and wondering what had happened. Thereafter, he wisely maintained his distance from Butter, yet the two weirdly stuck to one another, come what may.

For example, both would sit in the same room, go out to lie in the sun together, and sit in the same posture hour after hour, but rarely communicate. They looked like twins, albeit one thin and the other obese. Butter and Guchguch were born a year apart to different mothers and yet they bore a striking resemblance to one another.

Soon it was time for what we believed to be Butter's eleventh birthday party. I bought her a beautiful pink polka-dot dress for the occasion, and decided a dress rehearsal was in order so I could ensure it fit. I took the dress from the drawer and turned to Butter. Guchguch suddenly appeared out of nowhere and pushed Butter aside, earning himself a sharp retort from his frenemy.

But all of Guchguch's attention was on the pink polka dot dress in my hand. He nudged me. "When have you worn frocks, Guchguch? This is a dress worn by lady dogs." But he would not be dissuaded, barking and generally causing an uproar. "I think you might be a bit big for this dress, my dear," I told him, sympathy in my voice.

But he had obviously fallen for the dress. I gave in to his demands and reluctantly tugged it over his head. The dress barely fit him in the chest area, while his protruding belly stuck out comically on all sides. I could barely contain my laughter, but I couldn't hurt his feelings, so I assured him he looked marvelous!

At this point he got so excited he broke into a run wearing the undersized dress. Butter went ballistic and chased him down, demanding he return her beautiful gown to its rightful owner. By now I had given up and was rolling on the floor with laughter, the sheer comedic joy bringing tears to my eyes. I finally pulled myself together enough to stop Guchguch, who was aimlessly racing from one room to another to ensure everyone saw his costume. He finally tired enough to sit on the bed while I undressed him, and Butter made him promise never to set his eyes on her clothes again.

I could see the wheels turning in my boy's mind: if not clothes, then what about bedsheets? Maybe I could make my own dress, he apparently thought to himself. And so the sheets became Guchguch's next target. Butter made every attempt to keep law and order in the household, but alas, it fell on deaf ears in the case of her nemesis. Maa or I had to constantly intervene to prevent Guchguch from creating torn fragments that were eventually converted to napkins and duster cloths.

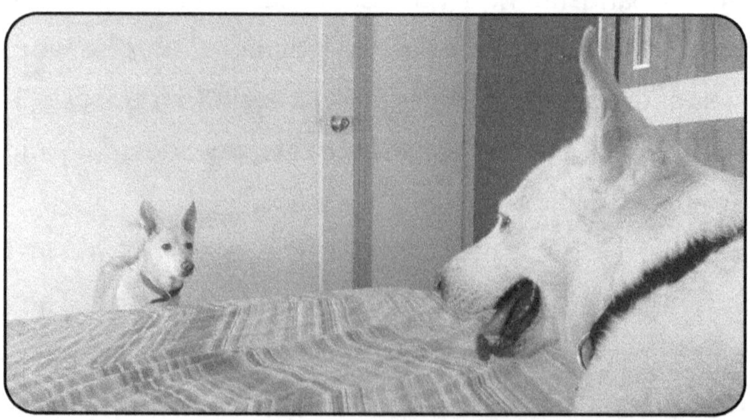

In fact, it is due to Guchguch's passion that one of our cupboards still holds his massive collection of "fashion artwork." To make matters worse, it was on one of our boy's bedsheet missions that my laptop unfortunately fell prey to his ministrations. Two tight kicks—as powerful as that of a mule—by Guchguch and my laptop was rushed to the computer engineer for recovery.

As he aged, Guchguch loved to sleep throughout the day and developed a protruding belly. With his two loves—food and his human mother (me)—and Butter for company, life was finally all good for Guchguch.

Before long, another habit Guchguch aspired to would leave Butter annoyed with her lieutenant. Guchguch liked to fit his rear end into the shrubs of the garden to defecate. While most of the defecated material became manure for the plants, some of it, occasionally, was left behind on top of the shrubs and looked like deformed and dehydrated brown flowers. Maa and I had to clear the lawn of those "special flowers" in order to avoid any embarrassment in front of the gardener.

The two did have some moments of solidarity, however. For instance, they delighted in chasing the feral cats who dropped by our place for a meal. While Butter was swift and agile and ran the cats off if she spotted them, Guchguch often slipped and fell during the chase, causing us to laugh with glee and the cats to roam freely while he was on patrol.

Though our two strong-willed dogs portrayed indifference or dislike towards one another, in reality they loved each other madly, almost like the characters of Tom & Jerry so many grew up watching. When either of them became unwell, the other would sit close by, wait for the other to recover, and begin their antics anew. They often struck a similar pose for the camera, and the three of us were a pack: Butter (the leader), me (the nanny to Butter), and Guchguch (the nanny's son). Butter and Guchguch joined each other one after the other over the rainbow bridge in a year's span.

Together they are giving a reason to smile to so many up there who wait for their loved ones. What remains with me today are the memories of them deeply etched into both my heart and the place they called their home.

Dr. Kuhu Roy is a nutritionist by profession and has been a proud mother to 50 precious less-adoptables in two decades: senior, blind, and/or paralyzed stray dogs.

She is also a Pet Loss Grief Specialist (India's first), providing no-fee grief support to the bereaved in India and across the globe under the aegis of her non-profit, Bridging Rainbows Foundation (bridgingrainbows.org), which is dedicated to Butter, a rescued dog.

DOES THIS DRESS MAKE MY BUTT LOOK BIG?

Um, guys?
Where'd
Everyone
Go?

Max Suckles, Stashes, and Splats

BY TAMIRA THAYNE

I live with one of "those cats." You know the ones…those whacked out moppets with crazy eyes and brains that "don't quite tick raight."

The day I acquired Max I thought gawd was looking down upon me and giving me a big ol' smile. Now I can only presume the big guy or gal in the sky was giving me the big ol' finger instead. *How rude!*

I thought Jeebus was better than that.

Anyway, so here I was, in need of a cat.

The cat distribution system had passed me over recently, and I found myself catless after Tootie left to explore the Rainbow Bridge.

Being catless is no bueno for me. The little devils very early on carved out a big section of my heart and replaced it with butt juice and cat litter detritus, and when they aren't within cuddling range you can color me bereft.

As long as I am able to hear them purr and rub my face through their soft little neck fur, my little corner of the world becomes almost bearable—which is an existence we can all aspire to.

My boy Max is truly one of a kind, though—just mostly not the fun kind.

I acquired Max, full name Max Stryker, from the local humane society, but not in the usual way. After we moved to West Virginia and got settled in, I decided it was well past time that I go in search of a kitty.

I moseyed my way along to the humane society, where I was greeted with the usual smells of the shelter as well as the usual salty countenances of those who worked or volunteered there.

I understood, though. Animal rescue is hard and overwhelmingly thankless; it's quite difficult to remain a font of good cheer in the face of all that suffering.

I perused the cat section, but to be honest I had my heart set on a kitten.

Selfishly. Just this once.

Joe had become fond of telling me that whatever cat(s) I adopted would most likely be my last; we'd crossed the 60-year-old Rubicon, and if they lived to be 18 years old, we'd be downright ancient at 78 by then.

Yikes! What a downer that man can be, what with all his truth-telling and such.

When you're active in rescue, you by default get "stuck" with the hard to adopt babies, especially cats. (Dogs are easier.) And I never minded, truly, but if this was one of the last cats I'd ever get to love, I wanted a kitten all my own.

As my luck would have it, all the kittens at the shelter were either suspiciously sick or already spoken for.

I hung my head and started to make my way out of the adoption area just as two young girls came in through the front door, a kitten clinging to the taller of the two.

She sheepishly walked up to the counter and asked if they were taking kittens. The staff member was as kind to her as she was to me—as in, **NOT AT ALL.** She grumpily told the girl she'd have to make an appointment if she wanted to relinquish the kitten; she couldn't just drop him or her off.

Since when do you need an appointment to drop an animal at a shelter? Probably since Covid, I reckon. That was about the time the whole world went insane and never flung itself back to the orbit that formerly passed for normal.

But I digress. So this young girl was left feeling just as upset and disappointed as I was, but now I'd spotted a tiny speck of sunlight peeking over my horizon.

Mayhap gawd had sent us both to the shelter at the same time for a reason? *It was divine providence, I tell ya.*

"Are you looking for a kitten?" the girl turned to me, a note of tenuous hope coloring her voice.

Hell, even if I wasn't, I would've had a hard time telling her no after watching her face fall just a moment prior.

"As a matter of fact, I am!" I replied, all smiles now on account of the equivalent amount of hope blossoming in my cat-litter-detritus-laden heart.

The ever-helpful shelter staff member cheerfully chimed in. "You can't make an animal exchange within our shelter. You'll need to take this conversation outside."

There I learned that the girl's name was Ally, and she'd found the brown tabby kitten after someone dumped him in her neighborhood. She already had a cat of her own and lived in a small apartment; her boyfriend was kicking up a fuss about the new acquisition, so she was desperately seeking a safe place for him to go.

The kitten, that is, not the boyfriend, although in a perfect world I suspect 'twould be the other way around.

I happily grasped the kitten in my aching mommy-claws-and-heart and collected her cell number so I could text her pics of the little guy in his new home.

I didn't want her to think she'd handed him off to an ax murderer, after all.

Max had tweaker eyes (you know, like he was a crack kitty or something) right from the get-go, but I thought it was all just part of the kittenhood package. Maybe the little guy had some rough early days and needed a safe space in which to calm down? *That I could provide.*

Our current couch is an L-shape with a rounded corner piece, and Max took to it like it was his own personal racetrack. Except every time he raced to where I sat in the recliner, he'd come to a screeching halt and hiss-spit at me. I thought it was hilarious at first, but after awhile, not gonna lie, it started to hurt my feelings.

"Max, I'm your MOM! Why do you keep hissing at me like I'm here to steal your last bite of kitty kibble?"

He gave me the tweaker eyeball, hissed, spit, and then took off for another round of the track.

I continued my efforts to "tame" this ostensibly domesticated being over the course of our first year, but the little monster continued to bite and scratch; he'd purr only when he was up to the no-good tasks of kneading my arms and suckling on my shirt.

Max the Suckler

Max has continued his suckling ways for all of his two years on the planet, with me being the only person in the family who will tolerate it. It goes without saying that I only do so because I'm his mommy and I'm pretty sure there are rules about such things.

Moms run in when every sane person runs out, that's my motto.

Here's the thing about Max's "little suckling issue": It hurts. A bloody lot. My forearms are now a crisscross of cat scars, and I finally took desperate measures to save myself by cutting up my thickest flannel pajama shirt and keeping half behind my pillow and half on the arm of my recliner.

Now when Max comes a'sucklin', I whip whichever arm he's targeting through the sleeve of the pajama shirt and it offers me an extra layer of protection against his paw daggers.

Desperate times and all that.

I believed the "divine intervention story" of how I'd acquired Max for almost a year, until I realized that Max wasn't just "in his kitten phase," or "growing out of all that crazy stuff."

It was time to face facts: Max was, indeed, two bricks shy of the normal cat load.

Gawd must hate me, and THAT's why he/she/they gave me Max.

Double rude, Jeebus.

Max the Stasher

Max soon acquired a brother from another mother, Mori

Max adopted a brother in brown tabby, Mori, who is as calm and laid back as Max is tweaky. Mori normally balances out the worst of Max's urges, but it will come as no surprise that on occasion Max enjoys a good bullying interlude with his little brother.

Mori rolls over and waits patiently for it to be over as Max gnaws at his ears and belly and sploots all over him. If I see it going beyond the boundaries of play, I intervene by stepping between the two, and then Max punishes me with a "surprise" attack bite or scratch to put me in my place.

Mori loves the soft multicolored yarn balls, and can be seen following me around the house with them to entice me into play. Max favors the little colored springs, probably because they're as "wired" as he is. When I toss them for him, he immediately carries them off to the basement, from whence they never reappear.

I told Joe, "That cat must have a stash of springs somewhere in the basement. Not like we'll ever find them down there, but keep your eye open just in case. I'm almost out!"

A few weeks later, I was in the basement when Max came hells-a-kitin' down the steps, pink spring clutched tightly in his mouth. I watched as he ran with purpose to the area Joe has fenced off, which consists of the water heater plus sundry wires and other paraphernalia the house needs to operate and the cats need to avoid.

Max carefully shoved his prize through the gaps in the wire fence and then gave it a whack with his paw to roll it under the piping. I hunkered down and peered beneath: there, feet away, rested a dozen or more springs!

"Max!" I teased, "What're you up to there? You got some kind of stash going on?"

"Don't look at me, crazy lady," Max scoffed. "As if I'd ever play with springs, let along stash them in that weird place. You've got the wrong guy."

"Uh-huh," I responded. "Well see about that."

I wandered upstairs to find the long grabby thing, (you know what I'm talking about) and brought it down to begin the excavation process.

Max, who still refused to admit he was the culprit, oversaw the entire operation, vowing silently to move his stash to a mom-free zone at his first available opportunity.

I've yet to discover said new location.

Oh, but I will, Maxxy boy. I will.

Max the Splatter

As if the afore-mentioned challenges weren't enough, Max is also one of those cats who needs a periodic anal gland expression.

If you're lucky enough to NOT know what this is, here's the official definition from the interwebs: *the manual, external, or internal pressure applied to a cat's small scent sacs located inside the rectum to remove built-up fluid.*

Um.

Yeah. I'm not doing that. (Right? Please say that's right...)

Normally, these sacs empty when a cat ejects a doody into the litter box as a gift for Mom or Dad. But some cats, like Max, either don't empty often enough on their own, or struggle to empty them at all.

Max's glands tend to release by accident if his personage is affronted in some fashion.

For example, Max often comes into the bed to suckle either in the middle of the night or bright and early in the a.m. He's incapable of quietly coming up and making himself comfortable, however. *Nooooo.* The boy has to announce himself with a series of meows that start off long and get more abbreviated as he winds down his solo.

This prolonged proclamation wakes both Joe and I (as intended), and I scramble to dig my suckle-arm-protector out from under my pillow and get it on before it's too late. I try to be quiet about it so Joe can get back to sleep, but Max isn't a cat to be woman-handled in any way, so it's like wrassling an ironing board into position.

On one recent morning, Max jumped into bed at 7:00 a.m., launching into his whole "WAKE UP, GUYS!" spiel. Joe hadn't been feeling well the night before, so I was especially sensitive to his need for sleep.

I got the shield into place and attempted to settle Max into position for his suckle. Not liking my intervention, the cat flipped his butt around and plopped it right beside Joe's pillow, something that would not go over well with the hubbins—this is a man who covers his side of the bed with a towel to protect himself from cat hair, for criminy's sake!

I stifled a laugh and again reached for Max, attempting to—**SILENTLY!**—remove him from the offending area and get on with the business at hand. Unfortunately, the trauma of me woman-handling Max proved to be too much for the boy; he **SPLATTED,** releasing his anal glands somewhere in the vicinity of Joe's pillow.

I froze, because there's no mistaking that odor.

It's a sickly yet almost-sweet stench, which reminds me to tell you that they make artificial vanilla from the anal glands of beavers. (I swear to you, look it up! *Anal glands. Beavers.* Just say no and spend the extra for the real thing. You're welcome for this life-saving tip.)

Where were we now…oh, right. Joe's pillow.

I was trying soooo hard to be quiet, I swear to you. But now I had miscellaneous goo **SOMEWHERE** in our bed and a husband who would freak the eff out if he knew.

The situation was dire, I tell ya! Dire.

I surreptitiously sniffed my sleeve, hoping it landed on my jammies and not where I was afraid it had. Max had the good grace to look embarrassed—*it happens when you plop fetid butt juice on Dad's side of the bed*—so he high-tailed it off to greener pastures to lick his wounds (and hopefully his bunghole, too.)

I was still furtively seeking the source of the horror when I spotted something: a small circle of yuk on the bedsheet, just behind Joe's back. *Oh, no!* I panicked. *How am I going to get that off without him noticing?*

I was debating whether I should get out of bed to grab a wipe when Joe rolled from his side onto his back and directly onto the circle of splat.

Yikes! Double yikes. I'm dead meat yikes, even.

It was then that I took the only avenue of action still available to me: **the cowardly one.** I jumped out of that bed like my pjs were on fire, grabbed my phone and glasses, and slithered out of the room, shutting the door behind me and the offending cat.

I would definitely be washing those sheets later.

P.S. Can someone make sure my husband never reads this tale? That's the last thing I need.

P.S.S. Mommy still loves you, Max. After all, there are rules about these things.

I'M IN
A BIT
OF A
PINCH

MORI FILES HIS
FIRST COMPLAINT
"This f**king guy.
Just layin' in there."
ABOUT LITTERBOX
WAIT TIMES

Removing a Ferocious Beast from your Bathroom

BY LORENA ESTEP

I awoke early one morning and thought I heard a noise in the kitchen. My husband, Chuck, was still asleep so I got up to investigate. This is always unwise according to the movies, but I didn't note anything suspicious, so I shrugged and decided to use the bathroom instead.

No sooner had I taken a seat than an unknown creature tore from behind the commode, moving quickly and close to the floor. I couldn't tell what it was, but I instinctively drew up my legs and released an ear-splitting shriek.

Chuck jumped from our bed and ran into the hall, confused and looking around for the threat. "What! What's going on?" he yelled, his neck on a swivel.

The monstrosity had been headed in his direction, but, startled by Chuck's arrival, turned and dashed back into the bathroom. There the confused creature was met with another blood-curdling scream and flailing legs, courtesy of yours truly.

Back into the hall he went, making a mad dash past the man in boxers and disappearing somewhere into the bedroom.

"Oh, no," Chuck moaned. "How will we ever get him out of there?"

We stood in the doorway, peering anxiously past the edge of the frame and hoping to get both a glimpse of our tormentor and an idea of how to remove him (or her, as the case may be) from the premises.

I knew I wasn't entering that room until whatever it was was gone!

"I know," I offered. "I'll bring the folding table down and use it to cut off the hallway. Then the only escape route will be down the steps to the door leading outside."

Chuck shrugged. "That might work, let's give it a try."

I ran to get the table and we successfully created a barricade, our confidence level rising. Next, Chuck went to the basement and reappeared with a broom handle, which he used to probe under all the accessible hiding spots.

Finally, our torturer flew out from under the bed and into the hallway, and it appeared our plan was heading for success.

It was then that my brain identified the usurper who'd introduced such chaos into our peaceful Saturday morning lie-about: a tiny and adorable little chipmunk!

My overreaction to the size and relative danger quotient of our houseguest didn't quell the scream that again ripped from my lungs as he scurried in my direction.

I'm pretty sure to his mind WE were the terrifying ones, because he immediately turned and slipped between Chuck's legs again and back into the bedroom.

"Stop screaming," Chucked yelled, oblivious to the irony. "You keep scaring him."

"I'll try not to," I replied, "but there's something about a darting form heading directly at me. It's unnerving!"

Chuck huffed and went back to prodding under the bed, at which point the chipmunk raced for the dresser. Suppressing my instinct to screech, I settled for high pitch but low volume. "There, under the dresser!"

For the next fifteen minutes, there ensued a back and forth between the hallway, the bed, and the dresser, and then finally Chuck was able to shut the bedroom door and nudge the chipmunk toward the open door and freedom just a few steps below.

For his part, the chippy noticeably perked up as the chill of the outdoors—and sense of his own home nearby—hit, and he stretched his tiny body to its full length, racing through the door and down the walk before hitting the grass and scurrying up the nearest tree.

FREEDOM!

We all expelled a much-needed sigh of relief. Guess there would be no lingering in bed this morning after all.

I looked at my husband. "Now that we're up, do you want to go to breakfast in town?"

I never was one to let a good breakfast opportunity pass me by.

Lorena Estep wrote from her home in the Pennsylvania mountains, and published stories in *Mature Living magazine, Writers' Journal, On the Line children's magazine, True Story magazine,* and others. She is the author of the following books available through online booksellers: *Puddles on the Floor, He Rode a Palomino, A Bridge to Somewhere,* and *Out of the Mist.*

CHAPEL
WELCOME
ALL CREEDS
ALL BREEDS
NO DOGMAS
ALLOWED

I'm just here to help ya, like always. You're welcome.

Don't Feed the Ghost Deer

BY TAMIRA THAYNE

Come to Texas! You'll love it here! Visit our lakes… oh. Never mind.

Moving day can be fraught for those of us who've spent any amount of time RVing. Is the next campground gonna be "hallelujah, here we come" amazing or "run for the hills" atrocious? Good, bad, better, or worse than the last?

Both Joe and I knew by this point in our travels to manage our expectations as we made the three-hour trip to our new two-week home. We were in the middle of our Texas era, afterall, and had concluded that much of the landscape herein can best be described as "it probably grows on ya."

But hold on, now, hear me out: this campground was on a LAKE, so it was bound to be better right outta the starting gate! We would be camping on Lake Medina, to be exact, which sounded both large and in-charge to my novice ears. I was convinced we were about to be held in some very capable lake arms.

I've rarely been so wrong.

We were told we could pick our own site, so we hightailed it to where the lake would be, should be, only to find miles of dry lakebed instead! Confused, I peered around, head swiveling left and right and left again, as I attempted to make sense of a lake that was just no longer there.

Well, hell.

According to the interwebs, "Medina Lake was the lowest it'd been since 2015. For months, the lake had been sinking lower and lower due to drought and irrigation. The century-old reservoir was only **6.5 percent full the prior month, having dropped 33 feet in a year."** *Yikes.*

I guess we wouldn't be camping by the lake then…unless one considered a ghost lake to his/her liking? I, for one, was then and still am opposed to ghost lakes, and I want to go on the record with that one. *Nothing good can come of a ghost lake, nosirree.* They've got to be overflowing with ghost pirates, ghost loch monsters, and other just-as-unsavory characters.

What the campground lacked in water, though, it more than made up for in deer, you know, of the cervidae variety. When Joe checked us in, they told him, "Don't feed the deer. They're so tame they'll walk right into your camper with you."

I didn't see the problem.

"Sweet, I'm in!" I sez to Joe, who assured me he didn't approve of deer in campers.

I ignored him to the best of my ability—like I always do when he rains on my animal parade—but I'm here to report that 200 apple carts later and not a single deer had been successfully lured into my camper for cuddles.

I now suspect those campground workers were liars, because what deer wouldn't be queueing around the block to cuddle with me? *[It's rhetorical, no need to answer that.]*

Once again, alas, I was doomed to love from afar.

STOP
COPYING
ME

The Tale of Tannerific

BY JOSEPH HORVATH

There once was a handsome mutt who was rescued from the end of a chain in North Carolina. He was dubbed Tanner when he was freed from his life of confinement, but I called him Tannerific because he was such an outgoing and friendly dog. He was being fostered by my girlfriend Tami and weighed around 60 pounds with medium-length fur in shades of brown, cream, and white.

What made this dog stand out to me from the many rescue stories I was privileged to be a part of was Tanner's claim to fame; it turns out that there was nary a fence built that could keep the dog in. The only ways to keep him inside a fence were to either stay in the yard with him or fortify all sides like you were guarding the gold at Fort Knox.

Dogs are like people in that the way they are raised and treated affects their mental well-being. They can have the same anxieties as humans without the benefit of being able to vocalize their internal pain or get help to deal with it. Tanner's issue was that he loved people and wanted to be with you so much that he would do whatever it took to get to you.

This type of fear is called separation anxiety and is quite common in dogs who spend their lives in solitude at the end of a chain or in a pen.

Tanner's aptitude for climbing fences was well-known to Tami before bringing him to her house in Pennsylvania. Her representative in North Carolina had worked with the family to build him a fence, but instead of bringing him inside and using the fence as a way for him to stretch his legs, they simply put him inside the fence and ignored him.

It wasn't long before his particular fence-climbing talent was discovered, because he soon removed himself from the fence each day and lounged on his owners' front porch, hoping they would bring him inside to be with them. They refused to do so and subsequently released him to rescue.

None of us had previously seen Tanner in action. Knowing that he was an escape artist, Tami ensured that Tanner had access to the yard with the six-foot fence rather than the yard with the four-foot sections. Both fenced yards had access to the inside of the house via doggie-doors, which allowed the dogs to safely come and go and they pleased.

The assumption was that Tanner would be content to hang out with the other dogs if we weren't around, and no longer have a need to climb the fence. Boy, was that assumption wrong!

The first time we left the house after we brought Tanner to Pennsylvania, we no sooner departed the driveway for the street when Tami noticed that Tanner was chasing us down! We stopped and took him back to the house, assuming it was just a one-off kind of thing.

Then we attempted to leave again. We were unfortunate enough to discover that it was not a one-off situation, because when we left the second time Tanner was once again following us before we'd managed to get out of the driveway.

He'd outfoxed us already.

Neither Tami nor I could figure out how he was getting out of a yard with a six-foot fence. We had to come up with a plan to see how Tanner was making his escape. We decided that I would hide in the trees in Tami's yard while she would say goodbye to Tanner and then start driving away.

It didn't take but a moment for Tanner to jump (literally) into action. He launched himself as high as he could onto the chain link fence and then climbed it, paw over paw, feet quickly catching the next metal "rung," just like a human would. When he reached the top, he vaulted over it and chased after Tami and the van.

To say I was amazed was an understatement. *I had never seen a dog with such dexterity before!* Luckily for us, Tanner was an easy dog to catch because, after all, he just wanted to be with people.

I did some research and figured that if I added another layer of fencing to the top that was angled 45-degrees inward (these are called welded wire leaners), Tanner wouldn't be able to get over the top. Yes, he could still climb, but ostensibly that last foot and therefore escape would be denied to him.

Materials were purchased and I put a lot of effort into making sure the fence was Tanner-proof. I spent most of a day cutting and connecting in the new sections of fence at an angle to the original fence. At the end of the day, I felt pretty confident I had put his wandering ways to bed.

Feeling deserving of a reward for a job well-done, Tami and I decided to go into town to catch a movie. However, within the first few seconds of exiting the driveway and heading up the hill in front of the house, Tanner was already out and following us. He had escaped once again!

Not only that, but I had been so confident in my success that

Tami would have fallen out of her seat laughing if she hadn't been buckled in.

Somehow it wasn't as funny to me.

Back to the house we went to catch the dog and get him back inside. Now we had to figure out how he'd done it since I had no inkling how he'd escaped my fixes. Once again, I hid in the trees while Tami said goodbye to Tanner and drove away.

Sure enough, the dog was out of the house and climbing the fence within moments, except when he got to the angled part, he squeezed himself through the tiniest section where the corners met up. The gap was so small that I figured a Tanner-sized dog would never be able to get through it.

He'd proven me wrong.

Back to work I went. More materials were used, more effort expended, but in the end I managed to close the gaps on all the corners of the yard. Time for another test!

I again hid in the woods while Tami did her part to ensure Tanner knew she was leaving. She drove away and I waited and watched…and…and…and…SUCCESS was mine! Despite the dog's best efforts—and he gave it his all—**Tanner had FINALLY been stymied and was unable to escape the yard.**

Now that we didn't have to worry about Tanner escaping, we felt much better about the situation. We made sure that Tanner received plenty of long walks so he had time to both interact with us and get some of that energy out.

The next step was to find the perfect home for Tanner, which happened rather quickly since he was such a sweet dog. While the organization normally preferred a fence for the dogs when they found a new home, we were concerned about him escaping most any fence. Would a new family put the effort into ensure their fence was Tanner-proof?

It was a risk. In this case, Tanner was adopted into a caring home by a single woman who lived in an apartment and worked from home. He'd lucked out, with constant companionship, long walks and runs with his mom, and no way to escape when she left the apartment.

Well, that's assuming he hadn't yet figured out how to unlock a door…

As a child of Hungarian immigrants, **Joseph Horvath** is a first-generation American who grew up in Pennsylvania and was immersed in the Hungarian culture until he joined the U.S. Air Force at the age of 18. He became a cryptologic linguist and later an imagery analyst until his retirement from the military.

Joseph is father to identical twin sons and became a grandfather in 2025. He holds a Master's degree in Geographic Information Systems and a Master's in Organizational Management. He continued his career supporting the U.S. Government for another 24 years before his final retirement in 2026.

Joseph enjoys hiking and traveling and has been to all 50 states and over 30 countries.

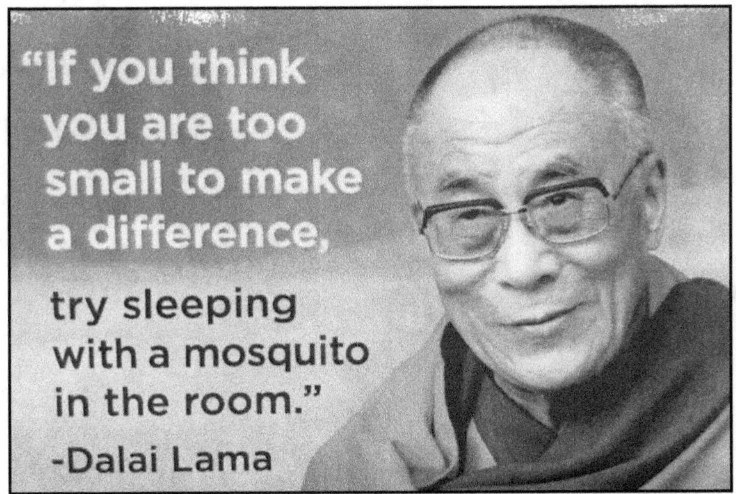
"If you think
you are too
small to make
a difference,
try sleeping
with a mosquito
in the room."
-Dalai Lama

I was told I could be a foot model? Where do I sign up.

When a Cat Cafe Has to Clarify that It's Not a Strip Joint

BY TAMIRA THAYNE

I guffawed when I saw the sign.

And then I wondered, "Hey, is this a clever joke or has the **Naughty Cat Cafe** been previously mistaken for an establishment of the night?"

I'm here to report that I don't know the answer to that question. *You're welcome.*

As we entered our fifth month of life in RV land, we found ourselves exploring Chattanooga, Tennessee, where I happened across a true gem in the wild. Or the city. *Whatever.*

There exists a fine line between animal educational opportunities and activities that further animal abuse or neglect, so not every animal story I ran into out there had the happy ending I craved.

This time it did, though.

As we tooled down the street, I was hit with a big **Naughty Cat Cafe** sign, and I said to my chauffeur, aka hubby, "Hold up there, mister. Imma need to take a look-see at this here establishment and ascertain if there's anything I need to experience there."

After all, Joe was there for the sightseeing—as was 50% of me—but the other 50% of Tamilina was there to cuddle animals, and cats are always #1 on the cuddle list. (Mostly because the deer, bears, foxes, and chippies won't let me. Rude.)

Many of my friends and family scoff amongst themselves about my unsecret Pokemon Go habit, but I'll have you know that I only discovered the Naughty Cat Cafe because it had a pokestop out front!

If you don't know—and odds are you don't—pokestops are disks you spin to get items you need for gameplay. They often pop up at interesting venues and landmarks, and someone local had been kind enough to put one at the Naughty Cat Cafe, which caught my attention. **So there, fam.** The game IS useful in everyday life after all. *[Don't say natty natty boo boo. Don't say it, Tami.]*

Along the curb out front, next to the **Not A Strip Club** sign, I found myself immediately smacked with the truth of the matter by a blaring *30 Cats Inside* sign. **I presume these words engender different reactions in humans of different types and temperaments, ranging from terror to indifference to ecstasy.**

I, for one, count myself amongst the percentage of the population who would run, don't walk (ok, I walked), immediately into that building. **"Sign me up for meeting each and every one of these 30 cats!"** I announced in my head as I sidled shyly up to the counter.

"Derp," I got out.

"Why hello, have you been here before?" asked the nice

fellow behind the counter.

"Derp. Cats?" I mustered, looking around suspiciously at a decidedly cat-free zone. *Had I been hornswaggled? Was this legit an establishment of the night…?*

The kindly gentleman then explained that I would need to pay $15.00 to see the cats *(say what now?)* but since they would be closing in 45 minutes I could get a 50% discount. And a "free" soda. *So there was that.*

Desperate to see what was behind that enticing door, I paid the man his $7.50—because never let it be said that I'm above paying to make new friends of the feline persuasion—but I did have a slightly disgruntled feeling about it all, not gonna lie.

Why don't cat cafes ask for donations instead of charging a fee to visit? For me it took away from the beauty of the experience. I'd have given them a $20 donation if they hadn't forced me into paying them an entry fee.

Meeting and loving and caring for companion animals like cats is a gift, both to them and to ourselves. When we are forced to pay for something we'd happily donate for, it adds a feeling of coercion—and these are not positive emotions I wanted to associate with interacting with cats.

Debbie Downer opinions aside, I ponied up the money and loved all 45-minutes of the experience. A spacious living room with accompanying fish tank (old school cat TV), welcomed me into the interior, and my eyes immediately latched onto the ten cats lounging on couches, chairs, tables, cat beds, and generally milling about in want of human attention.

Oh, and did I have plenty to give! I used a metal necklace chain to entice a few of them my way, where we exchanged names, email addies, and phone numbers so we could stay in touch later.

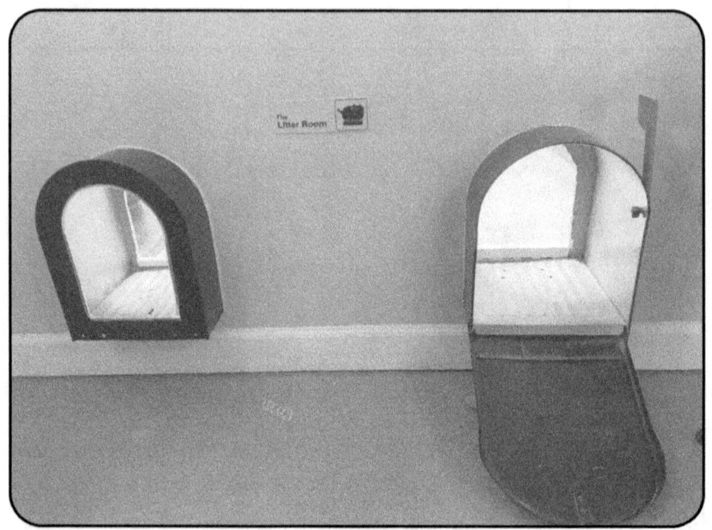

There was even a giant litter room that the cats entered through mailboxes embedded in the wall. Genius!

I left the Naughty Cat Cafe with zero doubt in my mind that the cats who landed there experienced safety, joy, love, and beauty while they awaited a forever home.

Hence making this experience one of the highlights of my Tennessee tour, and gifting me the added bonus of a guffaw or two in the process.

Score!

Whatever it is, I had nothing to do with it.

Beware of the Pongo

BY LIZ CASTERLIN

"Do you think we should get a goat?" is probably not the best question to ask while on a weekend getaway with your boyfriend, but ask it I did.

Mark looked at me liked I'd lost the last remnants of my mind.

But if he knew me at all, he would know I would not be deterred once an idea lodged itself in my brain.

I couldn't stop thinking about goats that whole day, so I took it upon myself to check out Craigslist to see if I could make my dream a reality.

To my surprise, I happened across the perfect gem—a baby

goat had lost his mother and needed a home ASAP. See, I could be a goat mom, and it had happened just like that! I was ecstatic.

On our way home, with Mark still shaking his head in disbelief, we made a detour to meet the baby who would become our beloved Pongo.

At first, Pongo struck us as friendly and low-maintenance. I remember the woman we got him from telling us we were leaving with a good one. As we pulled away, she yelled out, "Good luck! Oh, and he is LOUD."

I could understand why she hadn't led with that last remark, but I would soon discover she was far from wrong. The entire ride home the little goat screamed at the top of his lungs; I don't know about Mark, but I know I was regretting every life choice that had brought me to this point. I even wondered for a second if my parents were going to kill me when I showed up with such a noisy little beast.

We were about twenty-five minutes from our farm when we got pulled over by a police officer for speeding. As we cautiously rolled down the window, the officer couldn't help but laugh at the sight of me holding a screaming baby goat in the passenger seat. I remember him doing his best to yell over all the screaming, but even he finally gave up. "Well, you're getting off with a warning today, because it looks like you have to get that little guy somewhere pronto!"

That first night, before we could even venture inside my parents' house, we had to get Pongo quiet, which seemed like it would take a miracle. I found a duffel bag that was big enough for him to fit inside, similar to carrying a small dog in a purse.

Once Pongo got situated and zipped up, the security of this cocoon relaxed him and he slept the entire night away.

And, so, for the next two weeks, we somehow managed to keep him hidden from my parents. Then one day, my dad asked me, "Is that a sheep shrieking outside?"

I thought to myself, "Technically, I'm not lying if I say 'no,' because Pongo is a goat."

In the beginning, I took him to work with me every day, as I was lucky enough to work in a pet store and the customers loved him. He got so used to riding in the car and going for walks around the neighborhood with my dogs that I was convinced he thought of himself as a dog.

Pongo was such a presence that everyone who met him remembered him and his antics. He either made you smile and laugh or decide you never wanted a goat as long as you lived.

From ramming in my parents' screen door and jumping onto their couch, to peeing on the computer keyboard at my work and terrorizing all my clients' dogs on group pack walks, Pongo was one of a kind.

He's the only goat I ever met who could hang out on the dock and jump into a boat for a ride like he'd been doing it his whole life.

When Pongo got too big to continue his life as a local celebrity, we had to treat him like a real goat and get him a herd of his own, so we bought some property and moved our little family to a farm.

Boy, did Pongo have a lot to say about being treated like a goat.

Pongo is now gone, but his legacy remains. Through his descendants, and those of us who loved him and still share his stories, he will be treasured for years to come.

As a kid growing up in Brooklyn, **Liz Casterlin** never thought she would make her dream a reality. She dreamed of having lots of animals, especially horses, on a piece of property she could call her own.

Now she's a full-time dog trainer and owns a farm with her life partner, Mark. Pongo was her first step towards reaching that dream.

You can find Liz on Facebook at **jrk9training** and **barnyardpetzmobilepettingzoo**. Liz takes pride in her mobile petting zoo because they are all rescue animals who enjoy the company of humans and a safe environment in which to thrive.

I'm way too sexy for this thing called work

Keep Boo Safe or Die

BY TAMIRA THAYNE

How many parents naively, and often subconsciously, believe their children will grow up to be "just like them," because what could be more perfect than we are?

Don't answer that, Kids!

Since I'm what some folks would view an extreme animal lover, I assumed my two children would follow in my footsteps and together we'd elevate the status of animals worldwide to loving family members and yadda yadda yadda.

Bahahahahaha. What an idealistic, lofty-minded maroon I was, eh?

In today's reality, my son Rayne leans more toward "normal" human-animal caretaking situations—he adopted ONE cat and married a girl with ONE dog—whilst my daughter Brynn picked up on my cat motto (One cat? Nah…four or five is best) and then elevated her favorite feline to the world's loftiest pedestal, leaving the rest of us to mill about in the ghetto beneath.

His name was BooBoo, and Boo could do no wrong.

Woe to the tosser who even considered suggesting otherwise.

I rescued Boo when Brynn was but a wee lass; he was a nondescript brown tabby who at a glance seemed much like all the other brown tabbies of this world. It was three houses and many moons ago, and I needed an extroverted foster kitty to help me socialize a feral I wasn't making progress with.

I figured if I had another young male that was more social with humans, he could help bring the little orange kitty into the 21st century and hopefully a loving home.

I intended to find Boo a home too after he worked his miracle for Lion, but Brynn fell in love with the tabby's soft fur and loving demeanor, making it clear to the whole family that Boo was hers and we'd better be backing right off.

I initially took her solemn announcement with a grain of salt, because my daughter tended to declare each new foster dog or cat "hers"…until the next one came along and her flavor of the week changed again.

Little did I know that this time really WAS different, and Boo would become the biggest part of her life—and by extension ours—for the next 18 years.

Boo looks at me, flips me the catbird, and then leaps from the back deck, where Joe has created the perfect springboard by stacking firewood six feet up and then plonking plywood conveniently atop for a smooth landing and a manageable second leap to the ground.

"I can't lose Boo!" my mind frets as I spot the cat-who-should-be-bubble-wrapped flinging himself over the side of the deck and disappearing from sight.

Hades.

Brynn has driven to her father's house for the weekend, entrusting Saint Boo to Mom while she's gone, a dubious honor if ever there was one.

It's clear that Momma best be jumping the first train blowing its way through town and huffing itself to greener pastures if that cat manages to escape; someplace in another galaxy where a certain beautiful but scary 18-year-old could never find the unfortunate woman.

I rush to the end of the deck and peer over, just in time to see Boo slip around the corner of the house and head for the nearby carport.

Double hades.

If I didn't know better, I'd swear Boo'd bribed hubs to facilitate his prison break—except knowing Joe the way I do, I'm assured the answer is far simpler: it would never dawn on him that putting a woodpile mere feet from the back deck would enable a determined cat with a penchant for taking himself on walkabouts, or even a hungry bear set on emptying an out-of-reach bird feeder. *But that's a story for another day…*

I bring myself back to today's dilemma. *Boo!* Heart pounding, I grab shoes and race outside before forcing myself to a slow stroll. I know this cat, I know Boo: if I chase him, I'll get myself booted from his circle of trust. Instead, I have to pretend I've just gotten a hankering for a walk myself, having nothing to do with him.

"Funny meeting you out here, isn't it, Boo?"

Boo turns his back to me and races for the carport, assuming he'll give me the slip along the back wall as he's done in the past. But this time Joe's shenanigans have outwitted the cat instead of me: he's installed wire fencing along the bottom to keep the squirrels out, and that same wire is now keeping Boo in.

He's offended, yowling his displeasure.

I slowly edge inside the carport, assuming I won't catch him here because wily is his middle name; if the cat thinks he's trapped, he'll be an explosion of motion soon. Sure enough, he eyes me up, dismisses me as inferior, then feints to the side, bolting past me into the woods. **One easy point for the cat.**

Lucky for me, it's rained and Boo is a finicky boy. He picks his way daintily into the woods, protesting loudly that he's being monitored AND everything is wet…why is this escape party not as fun as he'd expected?

I turn in his direction, and he bounds toward the shed at the top of the hill, white rabbit feet a'flyin'. I laugh despite my irritation with my grandkitty, because although Boo is now an old man, you'd swear he was just a lad from that effortless and carefree bounce.

Happiness engenders happiness.

When I close in on the shed I stop pursuing and hang around

nearby, chatting to the cat in my softest animal coo. "What're ya thinkin' of doin' out here, Boo? Catchin' some birds? A few squirrels? A passel of bears, perhaps?"

He withholds reply, but eventually approaches me for affection, either in acquiescence to going back inside or because I'm wilier than he's expected. I'm going with Option 2, as my ego needs a little assuaging after being beaten down by a cat.

As soon as I'm confident enough in my catch, I nab him and race for the front door like he's the last remaining cat in a worldwide kittypocalypse and everyone wants a piece of him for themselves.

Back off, ya beeyotches!

I don't loosen my grip, I can't. I'm dead mom-meat if I lose this cat, and I know it. We finally make it the last 100 feet and inside the door with a modicum of face-ripping, leaving Boo to slouch off in disgust that he ever allowed me into his inner circle.

Whew! I flop onto the couch and relief has me giggling the last remnants of anxiety away.

There's something I don't know, though. Boo's picked up a secret weapon which he intends to use to his full advantage…he's eaten a ton of grass, and then gobbles some dry food for additional projectile ammo.

Revenge will be his…and especially sweet!

It's Christmas Day. Brynn is living with her boyfriend in town, but has asked me to watch Boo while she visits her dad, dropping him off the night before.

Except the next morning I can't find him anywhere!

Cue maternal panic. Again.

There's just Joe and I this Christmas, so our plan is simple: make a nice breakfast, open a few gifts, and then cart ourselves to the movies, where we will be enveloped within the holly-filled arms of a dark theatre, salty popcorn, and a frosty beverage.

I could see our perfect plan slipping away...

"I can't leave here until I find Boo!" I fret. "What if he managed to slip past one of us when the door was open? What if he's out in those bitter cold woods with the starving coyotes and they're drawing straws over who gets his most delicious body parts as we speak?"

Joe can see the meltdown is fully underway and he's all about self-preservation, so we abandon our gifts to the hunt for a wayward cat and hope we can find him in time to make the movie.

We call. We search. Outside. Inside. Deck. Porch. Basement. Storage area. Repeat.

But there's nothing. Not a sign of him, not a peep, not a reply.

I finally exhaust the reservoirs of my panic pockets with this cat, and a calm overtakes me. What if the little monster is just hiding somewhere to torture me?

The longer I think on it, the more plausible it seems that he's been inside all along, and I finally calm enough to remember he's done this kind of thing before.

"Honey!" I yell to where Joe is once again trolling the basement storage area. "Let's just go to the movies. Maybe he'll magically appear by the time we get home."

I try extra hard not to think about him while we're gone; and, sure enough, when we walk back through our door four hours later, there's Boo laying placidly on the couch with his buddies Una and Tootie.

He looks at me. I look at him. He blinks, I blink, and with that we seal the deal to never inform his mommy of this little episode.

It's better this way.

Trust me.

Let sleeping puppies lie
...trust me.

Saving Slither

BY **MARTHA MOSLEY**

"I guess we'll have to kill him," said my kind-hearted husband. As I looked at the skinny little snake stuck to the glue trap, it was hard to imagine an alternative.

We believe glue traps are inhumane and would never use one ourselves. We had specifically told our exterminator to avoid them, but a substitute worker had come that day, and this was the result.

A baby pine snake was stuck in the trap.

People who think that New Jersey is all urban development are seriously mistaken. The Pine Barrens where we live boasts a million acres of preserved land, with many rare plants and animals calling it home. Though there are other species of pine snakes, the northern pine snake cannot be found anywhere else in the world.

And we were about to kill one.

That it was endangered didn't matter to us as much as the fact that we had hurt an innocent creature. We wanted to make things right in any way that we could.

We decided we HAD to try to save the little snake instead.

My husband carried the glue trap, the snake's tail dangling, to a retaining wall that ran along our driveway. The Dawn commercial that shows baby ducks being rescued and cleaned after oil spills came to mind, so we decided if it was works for ducks, surely it would work for snakes? Armed with a butter knife, Dawn, and good intentions, we set to work.

My husband held the butter knife flat so as not to puncture the snake's tender underbelly, and began, millimeter by millimeter, to loosen the glue. As each small section was exposed, I scrubbed the area with the dishwashing soap.

Later I would learn that it would have been more efficient to simply use cooking oil to dissolve the glue, but we were clueless and just doing our best at the time. We kept at it.

The snake was remarkably cooperative. As he became more and more detached from the trap, he might have begun to struggle. Thankfully, he did not. A wriggling, writhing snake would have made a tricky situation even more complicated. Apparently, there are angels who watch over fools and snakes.

Finally, the little snake we'd grown to admire through our ordeal was FREE! As he quickly slithered away, I noticed that a tiny bit of remaining glue had caused a few pine chips to stick to his neck.

I have rarely seen snakes in our yard, and I'm very happy to keep it that way. However, if ever I do see one, I'll be sure to check his neck area for pine chips, just in case he's "our boy" coming to say hello.

Martha Mosley has spent a lifetime enjoying animals of all types and rescuing those who need it. Her children's book, **A Place for Grace,** is available on Amazon and recognizes the value of the seasoned love that older dogs offer. She also has had stories published in the *Chicken Soup for the Soul* series.

Martha lives in New Jersey with her husband Howard and adult offspring Michelle and Andrew. Their household has three dogs: Gigi a pit mix, Ella a border collie mix, and Sasha a dachshund.

She spends time reading, gardening, volunteering and walking their dogs.

GO ahead and touch it. I dare ya...

The Turtle Nanny

BY TAMIRA THAYNE

"**A**w, there goes my sweet Biscuit," I sez to myself, the cockerspaniels of my heart warming. "I love that little fluffy-tailed girl."

Biscuit is "my" fox, although she probably doesn't know it. Which, now that I'm thinkin' on it, is just as well, because she's a bit of an ashjole and I'm not sure I want to claim her as my own anyway after this mess.

You'll see...

"I wonder why she's out in broad daylight," I worried. "Is something wrong? And what's that white thing she's carrying in her mouth? I don't remember putting anything white in the yard."

Biscuit skipped across my yard, through the critter-hating neighbor's yard, and on to her cozy den, at least to my way of thinking. Yes, in Tami's imagination all the animals have peaceful critter lives and homes that keep them cozy and warm.

A mere moment later I watched Biscuit racing back into my yard, and now I WAS growing alarmed. "Why IS she out in the daytime? Doesn't she know she's nocturnal?"

From my window I could see the little red fox pawing the ground, but I couldn't make out what she was digging up.

I was gonna need to investigate, it appeared.

The sound of me opening the back door was enough to send Biscuit a-runnin', and when I spied with my own little eyes the naughty things she was up to? *I wanted to run too.*

But, alas, someone had to be the adult in the room. Or yard. *Whatever.*

Apparently, and unbeknownst to me, my back yard is the PERFECT location for turtles to dump off their young—in the form of eggs—and skedaddle back into the wilds from whence they came.

Most turtles, but definitely the box turtle I discovered making a deposit in my yard, like to find a hill near a stream or river and bury a metric crapton of eggs they've been hoarding in their bodies in a shallow hole, also known as a grave.

Great, now I had to be a turtle foster mom, too? I was off to a brilliant start! How many had I lost to Biscuit already?

"I didn't ask for this!" I whined, shaking my fist at the turtle, the fox, the master of the universe, and whoever else I could find to blame for this mess that I now had to clean up.

I wish I could make you magically believe that I'm ice cream cool during times of high stress, but we both know better.

Yeah, I panic, but at the same time I'm taking action, which likely resembles a drunken hummingbird flitting from the red flower to the orange and then maybe the pink is better and then the purple and oh, hell, where was I and changing its mind so many times that it smashes into the nearest garden wall.

That's how I roll in a crisis.

After ensuring Biscuit had absented the premises, I set about checking Boxty (the turtle's name, duh) for damages. She pulled back into her shell mighty fine as I approached, which is a good sign her mental faculties were still in working order.

She probably needed a shrink after her trauma, though, and so did I. Physically Boxty appeared fine, and I marveled at how such a small turtle could fit THAT many eggs of THAT size (about 1.5 inches long) inside her tiny turtle body. It's not like her turtle shell had any give or capability to expand?

I'd seen at least two eggs go to Biscuit heaven, and there were a couple more broken on the ground. Boxty was still presiding over her basinet, aka hole, and I sure as hades hoped she'd gotten everyone out before now because I needed to move her to safety.

Boxty's idea of safety and mine were two different things, and she was disgruntled when I moved her to the bottom of the yard and released her near the little stream bed.

I then raced (crawled) back up the mountainous hill in my backyard to where the remaining eggs looked at me forlornly. *Will you be our mommy?*

"No, I don't wanna be your turtle mommy!" I yelled quietly, in my head. "But I will…since you're hanging out in my yard and there's no one else around I can hornswaggle into it, is there?"

My daughter Brynn loves reptiles, so I texted her in a panic, "Help, I've become a turtle egg nanny! What do I do?" While I waited for her sage advice, I grabbed a small pot and my gardening tools and carefully dug around the visible eggs, lifting them out with any accompanying soil and depositing them into the pot.

I soon heard the ding of her response, which was good because I was already stumped on next steps.

"OK, Mom, whatever you do, don't dig the eggs up! If you turn them a different way than they are laying in the nest, the babies will die."

Eff. Double eff. Triple eff, even.

Worst. Turtle foster parent. Ever.

"But I already removed them from the ground!" I wailed, the gnashing of my teeth audible even through text.

"Well, if the turtle was still onsite, the eggs shouldn't be affixed to the side of the shell yet," she soothed. "I believe that happens around 18 hours or so in."

"So you're telling me there's a chance."

Woohoo. I'd take it.

She then sent me a video on how to protect turtle eggs from predators by *LEAVING THEM IN THE GROUND, TAMI,* and then building and installing a simple cage on top so the Biscuits of this world can't consume all your foster children before they even get a chance to find their own little creekside home.

My building arm of the Tami-Joe partnership, i.e. Joe, was at work, so I was forced into improvisation. I carefully laid the eggs back in the hole in approximately the same place I'd found them.

Six remained viable, although one seemed a little crushed on one side, so I had my doubts about its efficacy in the face of such a daunting future. *But who was I to decide its fate?*

As a temporary solution, I snagged a wood and metal fencing section from my dog fostering days out of our basement storage area, then placed it squarely over the newly re-buried eggs, using some rocks to hold it in place.

That evening, Joe and I came up with a plan and by day three he'd built our foster turtles their own little safety enclosure, complete with escape cutout for when they dug out and were ready to make their way into the world.

The interwebs informed me that the babies should incubate between 60-75 days, but it COULD be earlier, or it COULD be later. *Holy exacto, webbies!*

So for the next two months I waited, watched, and even pranced around in an old prom dress a few times hoping for a baby turtle birthday party. But nothing.

Disappointed, I placed a ring camera outside the cutout area for a couple weeks, but it kept getting knocked over by other animals.

It wasn't long after that I noticed "it," though…It appeared that someone—or multiple someones—had dug themselves out the top of the cage rather than using the escape hatch at the bottom.

Did my babies fledge and leave the nanny nest without me getting to even slobber all over them? Boo. *Boohoohoo.*

While I never got to see the baby turtles alive and well with my own peepers, I choose to believe that each and every one of those little foster eggs hatched, dug out, and as we speak are living happy and fulfilling turtle lives down at the stream.

It's how I get through the day.

RAINBOW BR
WEIGHT LIMIT
5 MILES AHEAD
SINGLE UNIT VEHICLES
5-AXLE 29T
6-AXLE 30T
7-AXLE 32T
THE RAINBOW BRIDGE HAS
WEIGHT LIMITS NOW?
THAT'S IT, WE'RE SUING!

Beasts and Balls

BY JOSEPH HORVATH

"Beast," aka Quest, was being fostered by my then-girl-friend Tamira Thayne, founder of Dogs Deserve Better. Despite his scary nickname, Beast was a friendly Akita who loved people and made you feel safer just being around him. I doubt there were too many nefarious characters willing to harm you when The Beast was around!

As a dog who'd suffered inhumane conditions much of his life, there was nothing Beast loved more than to go for walks with his pack. Tami believed in letting the dogs run and play in the wilds whenever possible, so she would take her ever-changing pack of foster dogs to the state forest near her Pennsylvania home as the opportunity presented itself.

If I happened to be visiting for the weekend, I would go with them to help corral the foster dogs when needed, often coming home with a tale or two to share at work the next week as a result. Beast would normally stay with us as we trekked the old logging road through the forest; but on this particularly beautiful autumn day, Beast ran on ahead and didn't immediately return.

The task fell to me to go out and scout for the dog, while Tami and her young daughter Brynn rested on a log by the creek watching the others sniff around and explore the water. After a fruitless 20 minutes or so of meandering and calling for Beast to no avail, I gave up and started the trek back to the pack.

Tami was yelling something as I approached, but I couldn't hear what she was saying over the brittle crunch of leaves underfoot. Assuming she was asking if I had found any signs of Beast, I shook my head and yelled back that I couldn't find him anywhere.

Without my knowledge—but hilariously visible to Tami and Brynn—Beast was making me out to be a liar of epic proportions. He'd trotted up from behind like he'd been there all along, and as he drew alongside me, I noticed there was something fairly large and red in his mouth. My heart dropped, and I thought, "Oh, no . . . what is that?"

I was afraid to look, but all too soon I learned that the dog was carrying an actual heart, ostensibly from what until recently had been a living being. Unbeknownst to us non-hunters in the pack, it was deer season in rural Pennsylvania, and Beast had come upon the discarded remains of a recently field-dressed deer. Beast—being a dog—decided he would grab himself a trophy and bring it back to us to show off his prize.

After I got over the shock of seeing a 130-lb. dog carrying a freshly removed heart, it occurred to me that I had to get Beast to put the heart down before we reached the other dogs. I also had to accomplish this without letting them know there was a bloody, smelly "something" for them to roll in nearby.

Tami and Brynn stepped up their distraction game with the rest of the dogs while I had a chat with Beast. To his credit, Beast grudgingly put the heart down when I asked and followed me to where they waited. We quickly got all the dogs headed in the opposite direction and congratulated ourselves: we were in the clear!

Or so we thought…

After we were well away from the location of the heart, we stopped at a larger creek not far from where we parked to let the dogs swim and play fetch. Bryn and Tami took turns throwing the ball into the stream for the dogs while I remained on high alert, keeping an eye out for bears or anything else untoward that might come our way. After just a few minutes, I looked around and realized that Beast had quietly disappeared again. Since I'd failed to find him the first time he strayed, we decided to remain at the stream in hopes he would make his way back shortly.

Ten minutes later Beast did indeed reappear; and, as luck would have it, he was not empty-mouthed this time either. Turns out he was gone the exact amount of time necessary to race back to the discarded deer parts, grab the most enticing appendage he could sniff out, and return to the creek so he wouldn't miss the action or be missed by the pack.

While we watched in horror, he dropped this new prize next to Brynn, ensuring the young girl wouldn't soon forget this particular woodsy adventure. Tami hastily pulled her daughter away from the whatever-it-was, and I, once again, got the nasty job of dealing with it.

I realized that Beast had delivered a body part so unexpected that I was wishing he had just gone back and grabbed the heart again instead. I am not privy to the inner workings of a dog's mind, but of all the parts that were probably available, Beast had chosen—drum-roll please—the penis and testicles.

Brynn looked at me questioningly, and I realized now I had a new problem on my hands: how to answer the inquiries of a 10-year-old girl I'd only known for eight months. I decided forthright was probably best, so I told her that they were in fact the penis and testicles of a male deer and hoped that would be the end of it.

I was almost proud of myself! There, it was done, quickly and painlessly. Time to move on.

Unfortunately for me, it was not the quick end to the conversation that I had hoped for, but the beginning of a discussion for which I was wholly unprepared. Instead of accepting my answer and going back to playing by the stream, she replied, "No, they aren't; they have hair on them."

I had raised two boys, so I'd never had the daughter experience. I felt confused, wondering why this young girl would even presume that they would be hairless? How did the conversation even go there?

Realizing I was completely out of my depth, I did the only smart thing a man like me could do: I ran. Not literally, of course, but I did call out, "we should probably be getting back now," as I turned tail and hastened to her mom's side.

My pride in my response now in tatters and her daughter's comeback unanswered, Tami and I quickly rounded up Beast and the rest of the pups and headed back to her house.

I later recounted the exchange to Tami and we both got a laugh out of it. It would seem that Brynn had compared the deer parts to the only male she'd seen, her brother when they were younger. At least the mystery was solved!

I, for one, would forever remember the day that a walk with The Beast turned into an awkward anatomy lesson . . . **one I hope to never repeat.**

As a child of Hungarian immigrants, **Joseph Horvath** is a first-generation American who grew up in Pennsylvania and was immersed in the Hungarian culture until he joined the U.S. Air Force at the age of 18. He became a cryptologic linguist and later an imagery analyst until his retirement from the military.

Joseph is father to identical twin sons and became a grandfather in 2025. He holds a Master's degree in Geographic Information Systems and a Master's in Organizational Management. He continued his career supporting the U.S. Government for another 24 years before his final retirement in 2026.

Joseph enjoys hiking and traveling and has been to all 50 states and over 30 countries.

DONT SHOOT.
I SWEAR I NEVER
TOUCHED YOUR
NACHOS.

Meeting the Elder Elkins

BY TAMIRA THAYNE

It's a Baby Elk. Blowing a raspberry. *Swoon.*

We came so close to missing it, missing a rare opportunity in the animal kingdom, and I'm here to tell you, "Don't be like us. Find the critters, the rare ones, the ones living their best lives in the wilds of this fine planet ... before it's too late and they're whisked away to safety by aliens smart enough to know humans destroy everything we touch."

Remember how I told you Joe and I bumble about when we travel? *It's true, we do.* We're lucky to grasp any critter sightings in our tiny clawed hands, because clueless isn't just an adjective but a way of life for us. Our normal plan of attack goes something like this: we hit our next campground, fight about setting up camp, set up camp, forget we're mad at each other, then grab some grub in a nearby town and scrounge the brochure racks for anything appealing.

I shudder to think how close we came to missing the Clan of the Elkins.

According to interweb experts [i.e., not me]:

"The Great Smoky Mountains National Park's largest animal, elk can weigh 700 pounds and reach a height of five feet at the shoulder. Elk were hunted to extinction in the area by the mid-1800s, but a successful 2001 reintroduction project brought them back to the park. Now, the population numbers as many as 200 elk."

That's right. Man does what man does, which is hunt critters to extinction without a thought as to what will happen when they're all gone. Then smarter folks, probably women, come along to take control of the sitcheashun: *"Look what you idiots have done now! You killed them all! Maroons, each and every last one of ya."*

So these smarter folks reintroduced the Elkin Clan to the park and the herd has made a new home for themselves, leaving the elk pre-rescued and ready for me to fawn over . . . just the way I like them.

But they weren't in the brochures!

We checked. Any animal establishment catches my eye, and I peruse brochures and the local interwebs to find ways to interact with animals that bring me happiness and don't cause them harm.

It was Joe's son Garrett who saved us from ourselves. Garrett and a few friends were staying in a cabin about 40 miles away from us near the national park, and we mentioned we'd drop by for a visit that Saturday evening.

But Garrett texted that they were going to take pictures of the elk instead, and I was immediately intrigued, one might even say on high alert.

"Elk, said the lad? Please, do go on…"

After seeing Garrett's photos and getting more info on where we needed to go to witness this miracle for ourselves, you can bet we'd parked our butts in that truck by noon and were heading to Cataloochee to hike and await the arrival of the Elkin Kings—and Queens—at the golden hour of dusk.

We arrived super early, so we took ourselves on a hike into the forest hoping we'd win the elk lotto and spot the elkins in their secret afternoon nap tents, thereby getting the jump on the other curious onlookers already lurking nearby.

That plan was a bust, but mere hours and a few snack breaks later we were finally rewarded with our first glimpse of an Elkin Queen. Lordy, but she was a big girl, and hanging out nearby was her much smaller but obviously adorable calf. *Squeeeee!*

I was mush after that, putty in her tiny elkin hooves. Momma didn't raise no fool, however, so even though there were no park rangers to quell the most blatant of human shenanigans, I wisely made no attempts to cuddle a baby elk and raise the ire of the elkin gawds.

I was a gd grownup, I'm tellin' ya.

Mommelk (see what I did there) kept her baby far away from the larger members of the herd, so we wandered further up the road in time to see males sparring and females grazing in the fields. Every last one of these heavenly beings simply ignored the hoards of staring humans and got on with the business of elk life in the same way they did every day.

Were they worth every smidgling of the afternoon wait for their arrival? Durn right they were. I even broke out the old school fancy camera with the long lens for this little soiree, and no regrets were noted.

In fact, I remembered our experience so fondly that I revisited with my friend Julia last year for a repeat pilgrimage, visions of the Elkin gawds prancing in our heads.

This go-round our first glimpse of an elk came earlier in the day, when a big-antlered bull rushed past, looking over his shoulder like he was being pursued by the spiciest of hell's minions.

We learned from another voyeur that we'd arrived during breeding season, so it would seem that lone bull had been bested by the Big Cheesebull, hence the necessity for fleeing the area. As we continued making our way up to the front of the herd, we indeed spotted Big Cheesebull himself, bugling and bullying his way through the female herd and brooking no tomfoolery within his harem.

We watched them for awhile, oohed and aahed at all the appropriate places, then Julia and I looked at each other and shrugged. "Men," we said, then we laughed and hauled butt out of there.

Back to our peaceful hotel room, our adult beverages, and our TV.

The perfect end to the perfect day.

And not a single male around.

CAN
YOU
SEE
ME
NOW?

HOW
BOUT
NOW?

NO!
Someone Gots a
Poopin' Issue

It's Nacho Kitten

BY TAMIRA THAYNE

Check your nachos before you leave Taco Bell, bell-oved readers! Nothing worse than getting home and discovering—horror of hors-de-vors—that something has run amok with your couch potato pleasures.

On this particular Sunday, I troll from the drive-up window to the nearest open parking spot to take a gander at my nacho order. Sure enough, I'm missing three toppings!

Grumble grumble grumble. Kvetch, kvetch, kvetch.

I reluctantly make the left to circle back around to the drive-thru lane, despite Whiny Tami's internal plea to just eat them as they are.

"No!" screams Couch-Potato Tami, who wants little more in life today than the perfect nacho combo, her recliner, and a happy movie so she can pretend the world isn't a giant bag of schize-coated triscuits.

It's then that I spot him. A tiny black form shoots from the bushes into the path of my SUV, pulling up short when he notices the giant white monstermobile bearing down on him.

If you know me, which you luckily don't, you know I'm about to lose my dang mind in 3-2-1. My window's down, so my gasp of terror—appropriate translation "awwwwww, a baby, a skinny baby, must save him pronto"—is loud and may have alerted him to a need to flee the area, stat.

If you're an animal lover, you know the gasp of which I speak.

I jerk the wheel into that spot in front of the dumpster where you're not supposed to park. EVER. I'm normally more of a rule follower, but not this time, nosirree, because KITTEN LIVES MATTER more than dumpster lives. *Obv.*

I'm brimming with overconfidence that the little skeleton boy will immediately jump into my arms, purring and gratefully rubbing his button nose against mine in a bid to eskimo-kiss the crap out of me; whereupon I'll break into a smile so beatific that the good lawd hisself would have to dig up some sunglasses to dampen the glow.

But none of that awesome-sauce happens.

At my gasp, said kitten turns and bolts back into a gaggle of shrubs, but not the cute kind that you can see through and around. No, this is the mother of all shrubbage, a veritable forest of firville. I glimpse his tiny tail disappearing into the largest, roundest hedge. *Fudge.*

Smiling, I swagger that way, positive I'm still fully in control of this rescue mission despite the miniscule setbacks.

"Step aside, Shrubbish! I have a kitten to save," I bellow, imaginary swashbuckling sword in hand. "Come along now, tiny baby. I've got this sorted. As a show of good faith, how about some canned food I carry for just such emergencies *[pats self on back]* in order to distract you with biological necessities while I swoop in and capture your kittenhood.

"Nothing to concern yourself with."

But no amount of "here, kitty kitty"-ing could convince said tiny black demon to give up his hiding space and "Ollie ollie in come free."

I begrudgingly acknowledge that this task is far more herculean than at first expected, and drive home with a lot more weighing on my mind than cold couch potato nachos.

By the time I pull into the driveway, I know I'll be going back, cat trap in hand. I've finally remembered that cats aren't easy to rescue, and *it more often than not involves a trap.* Derp.

The land of wishful thinking has given me the smackdown I mayhap deserved.

I enlist the help of my always-reluctant-but-begrudgingly-helpful hubby to ride back with me in case the kitten magically ceases its resistance to my charms.

When the little guy's still a no-show to my one-kitten ball, I set up a trap with a can of cat food and tuck it beside the mother-of-all-shrubbage, satisfied that it's not visible to random passersby.

I then trudge into the Taco Bell to let staff know about the kitten and the trap, hoping to cut off any unfortunate surprises such as my trap landing in that conveniently-placed dumpster.

I ask a girl at the counter if anyone there had seen a little black kitten, and I hit the jackpot in Kerry, a woman working the drive-thru window. *Yes!* Kerry'd seen the kitten a week prior and spent an hour in the rain trying to coax him out of hiding with no success.

Kerry is so excited by the prospect of catching the little guy that she immediately asks her boss to go on break and walks with me to where I'd set the trap, promising she'd check it a couple times before she got off work at midnight. *She also wants the kitten!*

Whew. This comes as a profound relief to me, as I am not in the market for a kitten, and I strongly believed the CDN (Cat Distribution Network) had mistakenly targeted ME when it was actually Kerry they were lookin' for.

Joe and I drive home, my mood more hopeful than an hour earlier.

I'd set the trap at 5:00 p.m., and imagined that Kerry would check it by 10:00 p.m. at the latest. But trust comes hard for me in this game, and fear swirls in and out of my mind. *What if she never checks it? What if he's in there right now, but has to wait hours for help? What if, what if, what if!!…*

By 7:00 p.m., I can't take it anymore and MUST drive back to the Bell to check for the kitten. While I fully acknowledge that there are many Tamis living in my head, most of these personas agree on one simple rule: animals are worthy of our help in whatever way we can give it.

For me, this means that when Anxiety Tami needs to go check the trap, Couch Potato Tami gets off her bootie and agrees to go take a look-see, pronto!

As I make the short drive back to town, it feels like Christmas morning—only with cats—and my tummy is all aflutter. *Would he or wouldn't he be…?*

Can I survive the disappointment if he isn't there, and how long would I wait before I came back to check again?

I park by the dumpster—in what is obviously now MY spot—and my heart thuds as I get out of the car. I can't see the trap from here, it's so well-tucked into the shrubbish, but I finally get close enough for a good look and…

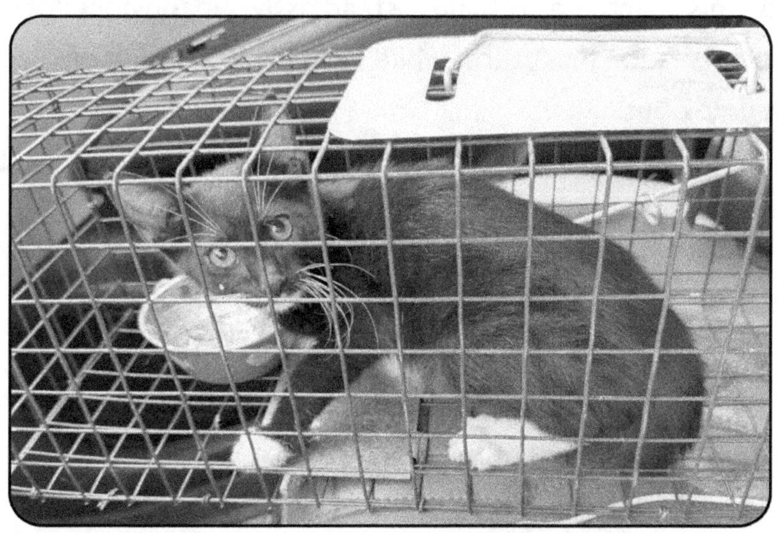

Oh. My. Dawg.
HE'S THERE!
He's in the trap.
This is SO MUCH BETTER than Christmas morning, y'all.
Fo' sho'.

Because with just a little effort on my part, I've been privileged to save a tiny life that would have ended very quickly due to the cruelties of our fellow human beings.

But enough laurel resting…

I yoink the trap up out of the shrubbish while the little dervish flips and flails, coating himself in the remaining cat food and hissing promises of much personal slaying to come. He sounds pretty serious about it, too.

Despite his unwavering belief that I'm the bad guy who has immediate plans to fillet and consume his scrawny little beehive, I coo reassuringly at him that I bear him no ill will. In fact, it's just the opposite!

For his part, he remains steadfastly unconvinced of my angelic plans for his future, while I'm riding the high of rescuing his grumpy butt.

The insults he's tossing my way roll right off.

As soon as we get home, I rush the trap into my guest bathroom which doubles as an animal rescue quarantine on occasions such as this. I know I'm gonna need a heavy-duty cleanup on aisle 2, and I'm not giving the still-roiling demon an opportunity to slip through my greedy little kitten-lovin' fingers. *No way, no how.*

I set up food, water, and bedding on the floor and a litter box in the tub. Then I give him a little time to himself to wind down before I commence doing one of the things I most enjoy: making new kitty friends.

Next, I text Kerry to let her know I'd come by to check the trap and we'd done it: **the Taco Bell kitten is now safe!**

She's as over the moon about it as I am, and she tells me how worried she's been since she'd spotted him out in the rain that night. She couldn't stop thinking about him.

She then asks if she can pick him up in the morning, but I tell her I'd feel more comfortable if we gave it 24-hours. She has two small children living with her, and the little guy is acting pretty feral so far. I need to evaluate him and get some worm and flea meds into him before I'd feel comfortable putting him into a home.

I check in on him a couple more times before bed, but he's still in no mood for any kind of kitten makeover or conversation, so I decide to give him the overnight and make another run at engaging him in the a.m.

The next morning I'm up by 7:00 a.m. and rushing to get dressed and to the guest bath to see how our Taco Bell baby has fared through the night.

But where is the little guy? I feel a moment of panic when I don't see him in his bed, and he's nowhere to be seen on the floor, tub, or sink either. *He couldn't have escaped, could he?*

Then I look up.

"Oh. Well, holy hades! How'd you get all the way up there?"

The three-pound kitten had somehow managed to climb the shower curtain, crawl over the shower head, and hunker down in the highest spot in the bathroom, the skinny window meant only to shed a little light.

My perfectly valid inquiry is met only with a hiss and a glare.

"Fair enough, Little Stinker, keep hating on your rescue buddy. But today you're not getting off so easy."

Flea meds are a top priority, since it's a pretty fair bet that he's being munched on by unsavory characters of the bug persuasion. Imma have to say a big "no thanks" to those particular houseguests. *Ew.*

But I realize worming needs to come first, and—given his scrawniness—one medicine at a time is probably safest.

Knowing that Kerry really wants to get her mom claws into the little guy, I spend the next day getting him well-fed and wormed, in addition to multiple efforts at socialization.

I'm not gonna say the boy is an easy nut to crack, but a mere 24-hours later I'm able to pick him up without fear of being bitten or scratched, and he even starts coming to ME for attention! *Score.*

It's then that I'm forced to have that little foster talk with myself that's happened many times in the past. "Don't get attached, Tami…there's a mom and two little kids anxiously awaiting the arrival of this little guy."

Love him.

Let him go.

My new-old mantra.

The next day, Joe and I drive TB (short for Taco Bell, since he's not my baby to name) to Kerry's apartment—with supplies like toys, kitten food, and bowls—and she agrees to keep him in her bathroom for the first night until his worm meds pass and he gets used to the litter box.

By the next morning I've got multiple panicked texts from Kerry. Apparently the worm medicine has found it's way through TB's system, and Kerry had the good fortune of waking to the poop-n-worm-pocalypse in her bathroom.

Yikes.

Is it wrong to think "better her than me?" Yeah, that's probably wrong. So of course I wouldn't think that.

Pffft. As if.

Kerry and I text a lot about TB and his well-being over the next couple weeks. Fortunately the poopocalypse is short-lived, his fleas are the next to go, and the kitten quickly bonds with her girls and sleeps wrapped around Kerry's head.

When I ask what she's named the kitten, her response slays.

"I named him Nacho, both because of where he was found, but also because of the girls' grandmother. She tried to name him, and I was like 'Nope. *His name's Nacho. As in "Not-Yo-Cat."*

"The girls will never call him anything else."

Nacho it is.

Take that, grandma.

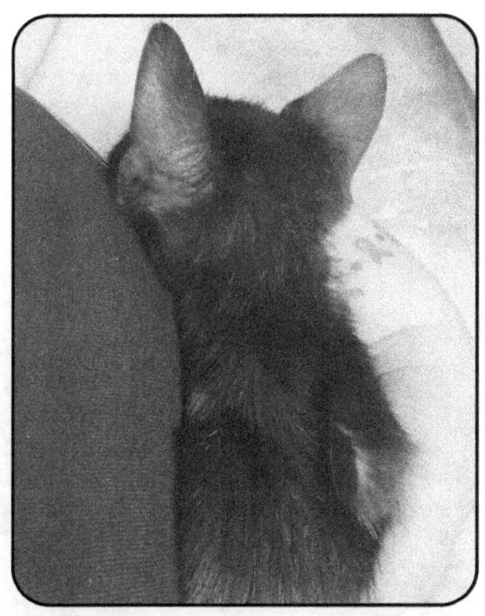

HEY LOOK...
A MENU !
ILUVBEARS

How to Rescue a Bear

BY TAMIRA THAYNE

The internet is brimming with How-To's, for everything from how to gently remove that ever-so-painful hangnail to how to climb Mt. Kilimanjaro in three hours and twenty-nine minutes….I may have made that last part up. It probably takes longer than that, right? **Who knows.**

In my ever-expanding quest to show the world how helpful I too can be, I thought I would join these do-gooder folks by writing a guide on how to rescue a bear.

A black one, to be exact.

My husband—who likes to consider himself oh, so helpful— pointed out that maybe this piece should be called "How NOT to Rescue a Bear" instead. But we won't deal with his negativity right now.

Onward and upward, pip pip cheerio, and all that good stuff.

Step One: Move to the Woods

This one could be seen as self-explanatory, because you can hardly rescue a bear from a New York City tenement building. But I thought it prudent, even wise, to advise that if you were truly in the market for rescuing a bear, you would want to move to a place they are known to frequent.

The black ones, in Virginia at least, are partial to mountains, rivers and lakes, and woods.

I, as chance would have it, am in a prime location for bear rescuing. [Pats herself on the back, amazed at her skill and forethought.] I dwell along a river that gets its humble beginnings in the Blue Ridge Mountains, and black bears often shamble on by looking to satisfy their next snack-attack, causing me to alternately: a. squeal in delight and run for the camera, or b. scream like a girly-mon and run in the opposite direction.

Whether I choose a. or b. as a course of action simply depends on whether I'm safely ensconced INSIDE my home and gazing out upon their bear majesty, or loose in the wilds with them—which to my lizard-brain puts me on the menu as their next tasty treat.

Yes, if one logically steps back at this point in our conversation, he or she could argue that I would be more like a four-course meal than a morsel, but there's no need to be mean. And, you're getting sidetracked.

For those indeed looking to me for expert advice, I'm pretty sure you're NOT supposed to run from bears. Which brings us to our next step.

Step Two: Google Whether You Should Run From Bears

I love the mountains and woods and rivers, and feel more at peace when I'm living out in nature. But I also have a healthy respect for [translation: abject fear of] any critters that can take me out. This goes back to the aforementioned lizard-brain, and includes but is not limited to: bears, packs of wild coyotes [as opposed to the tame ones, which are probably nice], poisonous snakes, and last but never least, ticks.

Ticks! Those little buggers will annihilate you without a shred of remorse.

And they're small, so you don't see them sidling up your pant leg and weaseling their way into your navel where you find their dead and shriveled carcasses months later when you actually remember to take a deep dive in search of fuzz buildup. Not that this has ever happened to me. *Ew.*

But I digress. *Where was I?*

Because I live in the woods, I spend a fair amount of time googling pictures of copperheads and rattlesnakes, hoping to be fully in the know that I'm about to die BEFORE they sink their fangs into my exposed calf. I also research black bears in case I come face to face with one—which is likely—and all my fan favorite childhood nightmares feature a bear breaking down my door, chasing me through my home, and eventually obliterating me. True story.

Unfortunately for me, my mind is like one of those plastic sieves as opposed to the metal ones, because it retains the big stuff while the small factoids slip right on by and down the drain before I even realize I'm leaking. I nod sagely to myself as I peruse the advice of actual experts, and then immediately forget [look, squirrel] what said experts have advised me to do.

If you move to the woods, try to be wiser than me.

In order to assist both of us again, I have just made another google pass using the phrase "should you run from bears."

I told you I was helpful.

I can now confirm that the experts (again, NOT me, we cannot emphasize that enough) at the National Park Service insist we NOT run upon spotting a bear. Apparently, like dogs, our girly-mon flailing and wailing greatly increases the odds the bear will see us as some yummy preylike treat and will give chase accordingly.

If this happens, let's not kid ourselves that the odds are in our favor. The Park Service maintains that bears can run as fast—

both uphill and down, mind you—as a racehorse. That's very comforting, no?

NO! It's not comforting in the least, Park Service.

I can't speak for you, but I'm no match for a speeding bear.

I only live in the general vicinity of Black Bears, thank dog, but if you live near the more Grizzly kind? MOVE! Right now. Don't wait.

That's my best, and therefore sagest, advice.

Step Three: Witness the Presence of an Injured Bear

This one, again, could be labeled by those in the know as self-explanatory. But not everyone has that laser-like focus when it comes to bear rescue, so I want to be very thorough in laying out the process.

After all, one would hardly have a need to rescue a bear that is a perfect specimen of bearhood and minding his or her own bear business. That's just a waste of valuable resources on the parts of both parties involved.

Before you skeptically question whether I actually completed Step Three, I shall set your mind at ease: of course I did…how do you think I recognized it as a necessary step in your Black Bear Rescue Plan?

From my living room and kitchen, we're lucky enough to have six full-length sliding doors and/or windows facing the river, because this is the area where all the cool, woodsy critters like to hang out. One summer evening I was minding my own business—[translation: minding their business, sometimes with binoculars like any good neighbor]—when a black bear happened on the scene.

I was initially tres excited [see INSIDE reaction] that she was gracing us with her beautiful bear presence, until I realized that her left rear foot wasn't behaving as said foot should.

Cue Step Four…

Step Four: Throw a Fit, Repeating "Oh God, Oh God, Oh God" While Holding your Hand over your Mouth, Wail at First Quietly and then Ratchet it up to Shrilly, and Pace About the Room Quicker and Quicker While Your Significant Other Looks About for an Escape Route

Admittedly, this step isn't all that helpful, and you can skip it if you're one of those together types who doesn't need to throw yourself to the ground, blubber, and gnash your teeth before pulling up your big girl panties.

Showoff.

For the rest of us, though, Step Four is a brief but necessary respite before dealing with the facts before our eyes, as we rail at a system we're sure is set up to destroy our last tenuous grip on sanity.

This blatant and ill-fated attempt at denial is often short-lived, and soon we come to grips with reality, which goes something like this: "Oh, **DOODOO CACCA**. There's an injured bear before me, and no one to help her but me. Whatever shall I do?"

Step Five: Toss Peanut Butter Sammies Like Candy from a Parade Float, aka, Don't Feed the Bears!

While one is left to ponder the challenge before us—which, to remind you, is that a bear is injured and you're the ONLY help around—it dawns on you that you can't think well on an empty stomach. The only solution? Make at least three or four peanut butter sandwiches. Stat!

After all, you need sustenance for the grueling feat ahead.

No, they're not for the bear. What do you take me for, an idiot? They're for YOU. You're hungry.

Everyone knows you're not supposed to feed bears. *Why?* Because then they come back! And who wants that? Duh, no one. [Looks about suspiciously.]

Once you've slapped some peanut butter onto some of your hubby's bread since yours is gluten free and EXPENSIVE, you still pretend this bucket o'sammies is for you in order to ward off the inevitable "Don't Feed the Bears" lectures.

If you've played your cards right, by this point your significant other is shaking his or her or their head, grumbling, and huffing out of the room. *Whew, what a relief!* That little pressing problem is solved and you're now free to take the appropriate—and obviously necessary—steps.

If you're lucky and said injured bear is still around after all the commotion, you slip to the sliding glass door, ease it open (critters in the wilds can be VERY skittish), and toss one or four of the sammies outside. In the general direction of the bear.

So you can BOTH think more clearly.

No, I don't DELIBERATELY feed bears . . . . I mean, there was that time with the bluebird house (that didn't end well), and that time or three with the bird feeders (those didn't end well), and that time or ten thousand with the dog food I randomly hurled over my back railing for whoever's in the neighborhood and feeling a bit peckish.

Don't be judgy. I simply enjoy throwing parties for my neighbors! It's not my fault all my neighbors are animals. I mean, everyone knows you can't have a good party without FOOD. I'm not going to a party without some eats. Are you? No. No you're not.

If you're lucky and the bear hasn't decided by this point that you're obviously a bear murderer and run screaming and dragging her useless limb back into the woods, she will have herself a little PB snack, and you can pat yourself on the back for a job well done.

At least she's not in immediate danger of starvation.

Now you can go stress-eat a few (hundred) cookies and ten (million) candy bars while you ponder the immensity of the challenge before you.

Step Five: Name the Bear So You Don't GET ATTACHED

When you've got a bear in mind to rescue, might I suggest that you name her first? That way, when everything goes south, you have a name to cry into your pillow at night.

I went with Cherry Beary. Why? Because Care Bear was already taken, of course.

Don't worry, though, I'm sure there are still plenty of silly and childish names left for you to ponder so you'll have one at the ready for your own personal bear rescue adventure.

Heck, you can even borrow mine. I doubt Cherry will mind…

Step Six: Decide the Authorities
are Probably the REAL Bear Murderers
—You Can Handle This On Your Own

Yeah, this step may not SEEM like the best idea on its surface, but in my defense, I spent 13 years in the animal rescue world. During said time, it became readily apparent that while about 50% of animal authorities are lovely and helpful to both the animals and animal rescuers, the other 50% would prefer to arrest YOU for opening your trap, kill the critter, and call it a day.

Could I really trust Cherry's very life to what amounted to a toss of the coin? No! No I could NOT.

How hard could it be to just rescue and magically heal a bear tootsie all on my own without any of the supplies or know-how one might need for the daunting task of bear fixing?

After all, I knew how to rescue a chained dog, my former area of animal expertise, which went something like this:

1. Stick hand out to dog, notice if he/she rips it off.

2. Hand intact? Remove dog from chain and drive to the doggy doctor. [Hand not intact? Drive yourself to the ER with your one remaining hand…which goes without saying, since you can hardly drive with the missing one.]

3. Assuming Step 2 ends well, take dog home, nourish, and bathe him or her or them.

4. Attempt to house and people train. [This could take a while.]

5. If/and/or when successful, find new, inside, home and family for the bright, shiny new lovebug you've created.

Presto! No authority interaction needed.

Oh, right. But I couldn't do ANY of those things with Cherry, could I? No.

We were both doomed!

Step Seven: Continue NOT Feeding the Injured Bear While You Plot and Scheme

Obviously, some rescue missions cannot be accomplished overnight. Rescuing a bear appears to be one of them. Deep thought and planning must go into a venture of this magnitude.

At this point, I advise you to keep the binoculars handy so a bear dragging a hind limb is easily spotted, a peanut butter sammy assembly line of one can be immediately instituted, and you can sleep better knowing that said bear will survive another day while you continue to mull over the necessary rescue plans.

I shouldn't have to remind you that during this period, it's to be hoped that one's partner is otherwise engaged in internet perusal, video game playing, or some other benign pastime due to the continued loss of bread and grueling pileup of lectures.

Step Eight: Whatever you do, DO NOT Look Out the Front Door at Night

You looked, didn't you? *Why does no one ever listen to me?*

Well then, you had it coming. Take it from me: if you spend too much time peering outside in the dark, you're bound to see things you wish you could unsee.

For instance—hypothethically-speaking of course—say you were passing by your front door (which has this tiny sliver of a window next to it) and you just happen to notice the motion light flicker on at the carport.

Curious, you stop and take a little look-see thataway, upon which time you spot Cherry Beary stumbling past the oak tree headed for the back yard where treats magically appear.

"Aw," you say to yourself. "Maybe I should go make some treats magically appear." *As one does.*

But THEN, instead of wisely heading immediately for the kitchen, your eyes are still glued to the motion light because you can't help but notice that right BEHIND Cherry, there's a MASSIVE—and presumably MALE—bear following her like Trump on Hillary at that one debate. [Don't pretend you don't know what I'm talking about. Yeah, like THAT.]

At which point, if you're a normal human, you panic and scramble for a hiding spot, even if you're INSIDE THE HOUSE. Because now King Kong Jr. is stalking Cherry Beary, who—let's face it—was already proving tricky enough to rescue.

And he's RIGHT OUTSIDE YOUR DOOR!

You didn't sign up for this. No sir-eee.

Plus, not only is your lizard-brain dragging you behind the couch, but your eyes are frantically searching for your significant other because you must—at all costs—strive to LOOK NORMAL while also keeping the evidence of King Kong Jr. from him/her/them. As a very wise bear rescuer, you're quick to recognize that this new development will only exacerbate the buildup of rebukes and therefore your headaches. The "I told you so's" can also be very annoying.

Don't worry, though. I'm sure it will all look better in the light of day!

Step Nine: Notice King Kong Jr. Still Hanging Around in the Light of Day. Things Aren't Better. Be Brave and Yell at Him to Go Away from the Safety of your Balcony

By now you've probably failed in your mission to keep your significant other (S.O.) in the dark about your little escalating bear problem. It happens. Shake it off and come up with plan J, K, or Z, wherever you've landed in the alphabet by now.

After all, your S.O. has to go to work sometime, right? You'll get it all fixed up while they're gone and there's no one raining on your bear rescue parade. Let's face it, these folks are bringing you [or me as the case may be] down!

With your S.O. out of the picture, the next time you see Cherry and her stalker who can't take "No, my leg's falling off, this is not the time for a romantic liaison" for an answer, you'll be able to act quickly and decisively to ride to the rescue of your bear damsel in distress.

Hopefully you have a back deck (without steps, a very important feature) from which to yell at a Big Boy Black Bear. The lack of steps definitely adds to one's bravery and the odds you might live to see another sunrise.

Might I suggest something like this: *"Hey, you leave her alone, you big brute! Yes, You! Now git!"* Or something equally creative.

At which point King Kong Jr. will probably stand on his back legs in order to get a better look at the fool who dares to challenge him for Cherry's paw. [One of the good front ones, not the one we're ignoring in the back.]

Unimpressed, he'll probably plop back down on all fours, give a little chuff and fake charge in your general direction, and then proceed to ignore you like the gnat he takes you for.

Of all the nerve! How DARE he!

Although, let's face it, bears can be rude like that. Not that it happened to me…but if it did, I'd probably be pretty unprepared to take the verbal assault further, or escalate it to physical violence against a 500-lb. bear. But you do you.

Once you've reminded him who's boss (him, obviously), toss a few peanut butter sammies to Cherry—some of which King Kong Jr. will easily intercept—and pretend you meant to feed him all along too. Because of course you did . . . this is one argument you ain't winnin', my friend.

As one very intelligent bear advocate told me, "a full bear is a happy bear…and no one wants an unhappy bear." She is a very wise woman. You can read more of the wisdom she imparted to me in the next step…

Step Ten: Realize You're an Idiot Who Really Needs Help. Yeah, It Took You Awhile, but the Important Thing Is You Got Here, Right?

Sometimes we are powerless against our addictions, such as the addiction to the absurd idea that we need no help to rescue bears. It's ok, thought, because admitting it is the first step! Now we can make some progress in a positive direction.

Of course your S.O. is out as a co-conspirator, that's already been determined. What you need now is a bear advocate, someone who loves bears and wants the best for them. And, more importantly, might actually offer you some helpful advice.

Where does one turn to find such a person? Facebook, of course . . . where one can find anything from rescue tips to an armed insurrection, it would seem.

A word of caution, however: you will learn the hard way that it is unwise to blurt out your rescue dilemmas on Facebook. I myself have never posted a photo of Cherry on this seemingly-benign social media application. Why? Because in doing so, you bring yourself more heartaches and unsolicited, random, ranting, ridiculous advice than you could ever dream of. I knew if I were to post a photo of Cherry's "little leg problem," I'd get comments along these lines:

"OMG, DO SOMETHING! NOW!" (Some people use all caps A LOT! Not me, of course…)

"I'm calling Animal Control on you! What have you done to that poor bear? Did you try to kill her? What's your address?"

"Why are you doing NOTHING. What is wrong with you?"

"Just get out the gun and shoot her. Want me to come do it? I'd love a free bear rug." [This comment comes not from one of your friends, but from some rando who happens upon your public post and knows the answer to any animal problem is to shoot first and never ask questions.]

You get the picture. That's a whole metric crapton of unhelpful comments and advice that will just cause you and Cherry Beary (if she has a Facebook page) more unwelcome stress.

It's not worth the headache. You could ask a generalized question instead, something along the lines of "Does anyone know a bear advocate on FB? Not for any specific REASON, mind you. Was just wondering."

This innocuous post doesn't set off alarm bells in the armchair rescuers, and you may actually get a name and contact info out of it.

You'll thank me later for this even-more-sager-than-ever advice.

I myself happened upon just such a bear advocate in this manner—someone who would probably prefer to remain unnamed in "my little rescue tale." I mean, who could blame her, what with all the sammy-throwing and bear-yelling and such? These may not be officially-sanctioned bear rescue techniques, after all.

Let's just say that upon befriending this much-needed shoulder upon which to cry, I sent my fellow—and infinitely more knowledgeable—bear advocate lots of photos and videos of Cherry and King Kong Jr., and we gushed and lamented and hand-wrung together as needed and appropriate. Then she in turn sent them to a bear biologist she is friendly with, who then gave us contact info for a bear biologist in Virginia.

Voila! Why didn't I think of that in the first place?

Step Eleven: Stop and Think About it for a Bit. Wallow in More Distrust of Authorities. What Does a Bear Biologist Do Anyway?

No, I'm seriously asking. What does a bear biologist do? I don't have the faintest. Sounds like a cushy job where you get paid to live in the woods and study the bears ambling by. How does one become this? You know they'd be lucky to have me in their corner.

On second thought, though, these bear biologists probably have to root through bear poop [also known as scat for my fellow bear biologist wanna-bes] to see what they eat and if they have diseases and other probably-very-scientific "stuff."

That part doesn't sound like a barrel of laughs to me, but you may enjoy such activities. No judgement.

So before heading in a direction which seemed suspiciously authority-laden, I once again consulted The Google, but this time for bear veterinarians and bear rehab facilities and the suchlike in my area. I reasoned that vets and rehab facilities probably didn't have nefarious intent when it came to Cherry's little foot problem, AND I could just ask questions, after all.

My location would remain secret, unless either I or The Google coughed up the salient details . . . [Never trust The Google, but that's a different article.]

Step Twelve: Learn Things You Wish You Didn't Know. Feel Despondent, Graduate from Cookies to Cakes and Pies. Wine of the Week Club, Anyone?

Things may be different in your neck of the bear woods, but I learned something real bad real fast that sent me into a baking frenzy: No one would help a bear in my state without the involvement of those I'd been studiously avoiding for the past week. I spoke to a vet with bear expertise and folks at a wildlife rehab who would be happy to help Cherry, EXCEPT—she had to be brought to them by the Virginia Department of Wildlife Resources.

Did your anxiety ratchet up just reading that? Yeah, mine too, simply from putting words to paper. Shudder. Not sure 'tis any way to make that guffawable: Cherry's continued health and well-being relied on an unknown. Something I could not control and had no say in.

I couldn't protect her if I reached out for help. The bottom line stung.

I have to admit, it took me three pieces of chocolate to impart these latest pearls of wisdom to you. I'm beginning to suspect either Cherry gave me an eating disorder or I had one long before that poor bear showed up.

Blame the injured bear, you say? Seems a little heartless, but desperate times and all.

Step Thirteen: Find New Big Girl Panties, As Yours Have Mysteriously Become Soiled. Dial the Bear Biologist with Cookie in Hand and Fear Clawing At your Innards

Alas, the moment of truth, the rescue-recipe ingredient you can no longer ignore if you want to get help for Cherry...that moment when the defecation hits the oscillating device.

Time to call the authorities. Gulp.

Might I suggest now as a good time to send up a plea to whatever gawds oversee bear tootsie dilemmas here on earth. I wanted Cherry to be healed and not harmed, which didn't seem too much to ask of the universe we all inhabit. I in no way, shape, or form wanted to feel responsible for her demise, but rather wanted a return to glorious bearhood for her.

These were high moral aspirations, indeed, but Cherry—and your bear too—deserve nothing but blue skies, cool rivers, and lots of safe eats and roaming territory to call their own. That's something we can all agree on, right? [Except that bear rug guy, who I'll probably meet in the seventh circle of hell after all this goes awry ...]

If you're in animal rescue, you unfortunately know that contact with authorities goes one of three ways:

1. Said big brass completely blows you off, which is frustrating as all get out and leaves both you and the animal in limbo.

2. The "experts" find a way to get YOU in trouble for whatever you've done or are doing to help the animal [not that the tossing of PB sammies comes to mind]. Or…

3. The professionals actually step up and get the animal the help he or she needs and deserves and everyone goes home happy.

It's a crap shoot.

So I rolled the dice on a hot summer day and picked up the phone. I don't mind tellin' ya' I was plum terrified, so I was.

I soon found myself on the line with a perfectly nice bear biologist who is employed by the state of Virginia Department of Wildlife Resources. Just the authorities I was [not] looking for. After explaining the situation and making the case for helping poor sweet Cherry, I texted him all the photos and video, and he promised he'd get back to me within 24 hours.

Hope blossomed. He was nice. Cherry was nice. *Maybe a match could be made after all?*

But hope has a way of cleaving our hearts into a million tiny turdlings when it ruptures, taking any modicum of faith in the system along with it. The next day I found whatever faith I'd managed to splootch together squished, squashed, even pulverized, like a PB sammy under King Kong Jr.'s bum.

The answer was No.

No? I couldn't understand.

Nevertheless, I persisted.

Why wouldn't they help her? *Couldn't they just trap her and remove or operate on her leg and then re-release her into the wild?*

His response? "I understand your frustration. Let me talk to my boss again and I'll let you know what she says tomorrow."

The wait was miserable and the odds not good, but I tried to dredge up some semblance of belief so the gawds of wretchedness didn't send a seagull to poop on my head, too. They're cruel like that.

[The gods of wretchedness, not seagulls. Seagulls are just rude, and I suspect enjoy nothing more than a new target upon which to splat.]

When the final Jeopardy bell rang the next day the state's answer was still NO. The reason? "The bear might become too tame."

Derp. *Isn't that what we have wildlife centers for, just in case that actually happens?* So then what DOES a bear biologist do if not try to help bears in his/her state? Study their pain and catalog it into some database somewhere? Admittedly, I was frustrated, angry, and sad.

These are the times one really needs a therapist on speed-dial. *I mean, how much baking can one person be expected to handle?*

Morose is a good, descriptive word which you might add to your mental dictionary in case your bear rescue goes as poorly as mine. For I was indeed exceedingly morose.

Bereft, even.

Step Fourteen: Throw Yourself Off the Back Deck. Realize It's Too Short of a Fall for You to Actually Die. Get Back Up and Drag Yourself Inside. Make Bear Some More Peanut Butter Sammies

So they wouldn't kill Cherry. *Yippee!* But they wouldn't help her either. *Sumbeyotches.* Cherry and I now found ourselves in that dreaded limbo, having nowhere to go but down.

With it becoming overwhelmingly obvious that my only bear rescue qualification is that of an adequate PB Sammy Maker, it was time to acknowledge that the odds were not good for my bear friend . . . who—let's face it—probably didn't even use the word "friend" when referencing me to her bear acquaintances.

I wouldn't either.

I therefore took the only avenue remaining open to me and descended directly into madness. I didn't pass GO or collect $200, but just skipped my sad little butt straight to the loony bin.

Or had I already landed there long ago and simply forgotten? *No matter.*

Step Fifteen: Wallow. Admit your Hubby was Right when He Said Your Story Should Be Titled "How NOT to Rescue a Bear." Make Said Admission Only to Yourself, Because There's No Sense Allowing Him to Gloat or Enjoy Himself in Any Way

Once you've sufficiently wallowed to gain 15 pounds in baked goods, been fired by your on-call therapist, and finished all the liquor in the pantry—if you're still married by this point—it's time to make peace with Cherry's inevitable demise, and chalk up this little adventure to the very long list of life's failures you've been conveniently disregarding since about the time you hit puberty.

Shove the list under the bed for later perusal [read: when Hades goes North Pole] and vow to never again rescue an animal. It's just too durn painful, and, face it, all these failures have really put a dent in your self-esteem. Which probably wasn't all that good in the first place.

Step Sixteen: Continue to Feed the Bears, Because Well, It's All You've Got

At this point you might as well take ownership of the fact that you're a hardcore bear feeder, and just get on with it. Rationalize it as being better than, say, a hardcore bear flasher. *That's just cruelty to animals right there: run bears, run!*

I personally found it liberating, because *screw you, Mr. Authority Man who won't help an injured animal, I'm FEEDING THIS BEAR. Boom!*

I also call this Passive-Aggressive Screaming into the Abyss Syndrome, of which I reckoned by now I was sportin' a full-blown case.

Take these actions only in the safety of your own home while flexing your pretend muscles and strutting about the kitchen in a fruitless attempt to regain some kind of personal empowerment.

Whatever you do—and you gotta trust me on this—do NOT make an angry social media rant about it, unless you're prepared to go the distance. Revisit Step Ten if you've misplaced this very important lesson.

Step Seventeen: See Less and Less of Cherry. Know the Inevitable is Coming. Cry on your New Bear Advocate Friend's Shoulder. Expect Her to Ghost You at Any Moment

While very engaged in and busy with my wallowing, I still managed to look for Cherry every day; I peered out each window as I passed, binocular straps grown into my neck rolls and eyes crossed from peering through the lenses.

Cherry-sightings became more and more infrequent, but when I did spot her beautiful bearness [as opposed to bareness, which would have been awkward], I'd rush to get my hands on goodies even more delicious than PB Sammies in hopes of enticing her to hang around.

I was a pitiful wretch, begging for just one more hit of Cherryness. I'd watch her with love in my eyes and sadness in my heart while she had herself a little snack and then carted her injured leg off to other, possibly less fraught, bear business.

As the days grew into weeks, I soon realized I hadn't seen "my" bear in a month. And then it became two.

I was sad, but—convinced of her demise—I told myself at least she wasn't suffering any longer. I'm sure there's a bear heaven for sweet bears like Cherry, and I pictured her up there frolicking with others of her kind, no limb dragging of any sort to hold her back from her favorite merrymaking pursuits.

I would never know how Cherry became injured, but I postulated that humans were somehow involved, since we as a species can't seem to keep our grimy mitts to ourselves.

It was obvious that we humans let her down in the end, and that bitter pill lodged in my gullet, our lack of kindness to animals enough to make even the most well-rounded animal advocate a teensy bit disenchanted with life on this planet.

I'm not speaking of myself here, of course. I'm nothing if not a spectacularly cheery and well-adjusted individual. *Dammit.*

Oops. I mean **DOODOO CACCA.**

I consoled myself with the "she's in a better place" platitude, hoping that soon I would come to believe this absurd load of poppycock, having given myself a sugar lobotomy and passed out in my backyard curled around my childhood teddy bear.

Nothing to see here, people. Move it along.

Step Eighteen: Realize You Have No Funny Ending for Your Story. Mull Over the Incredible Awkwardness of It All

When I set out to write a funny bear rescue story, I had only my experience with Cherry Beary to draw from. I was vividly aware that my tale had been beset by an unhappy ending, but I blithely ignored this teensy complication and started writing the story anyway.

As I neared the end, I found myself putting off the grand finale, because how could I tell my bear-rescue fans that I am indeed a fraud, a failure, and the bear I sought to rescue was dead? It was a dilemma, as one can imagine.

I remain confident that, if you are intrepid enough to undertake your own bear rescue, you will have more success than I due to my stunningly helpful—not to mention witty—

advice, and you have indeed learned from all my little faux pas-es.

Regardless, I prepared myself to hang my head in forever shame; mostly due to my bear rescue failure, yes, but a few other setbacks reared themselves from the recesses of my mind and were delighted to pile on in self-flagellation.

But then . . . but then. Well, you'll just never believe it…

Step Nineteen: Procrastinate so Long in Documenting Your Failure—I Mean Story—that Cherry Beary Comes Back to Life AND Manifests a Set of Cubs, Probably with that Knucklehead King Kong Jr. Who—Now That We Think On It— WAS Kinda Sexy for a Bear

I know, I know, I know! I couldn't believe it either.

I swear on my favorite kitty's dearly-departed soul, this is a true story. [Except for the part about dying and coming back to life. That's probably not true.] But the rest IS.

Cherry. Wasn't. Dead.

I HAD rescued a bear after all!

Take that, hubby, S.O., he, she, it, or they as the case may be.

Obviously, now is the perfect time for gloating, and might I recommend immediately casting aside all that woebegone moping in which you may have recently overindulged. Pulling out the natty-natty-boo-boo or nanny-nanny-boo-boo (I welcome both natty and nanny in my boo-booing) always works.

Back-patting is of course a must, as is amazement at the miraculous power of your PB Sammies.

How did it happen, you ask?

Well, there I was one late summer evening, minding my own business like I always do. In case you'd forgotten, my business mostly consists of minding the neighbors'—and by neighbors I mean animals—business, often with binoculars.

Then IT happened.

A momma bear wandered up from the river into the backyard with two cubs tagging along behind. And she had a lame back foot.

It was nigh on unbelievable.

Her. Back. Left. Foot. Was. Lame!

Cue Step Twenty . . .

Step Twenty: Squeeee! Quietly and Then More Loudly While Trying Not to Scare Bears Away, Repeating "Oh God, It's Her, Oh God, It's Her" While Holding your Hand over your Mouth, Pacing About the Room Quicker and Quicker While Your Significant Other Looks About for an Escape Route

I get it. Upon first glance Step Twenty strongly resembles Step Four, but don't be fooled: this time around the frantic flailing and squeeing on your part is for happy reasons instead of sad. Cherry Beary is not only alive, but she somehow managed to conceive and rear two beautiful baby cubs with that heathen King Kong Jr. after all!

Cherry's a miracle bear.

She's badass.

I mean, fur real, how could that poor injured girl even manage to um, you know, at a time like that? I was aghast and euphoric at the same time.

Despite my incredulosity, [it *should* be a word] the fact remained that for whatever reason Cherry had survived: she'd survived, and heck, almost thrived. Her back foot, while it couldn't be called normal, was not as debilitating as it had been the year prior. Cherry had made it through adversity meant to fell your average bear and even sprung herself a new family.

Cherry will always be my shero.

Step Twenty-One: Throw Peanut Butter Sammies Like Candy from a Parade Float, aka, Don't Feed the Bears!

Cherry was even more skittish now that she had cubs to protect, so she treed her babies and disappeared into the undergrowth when the PB Sammy Brigade wheeled into action and the door slipped open far enough for the toss.

While I was panicked that she wouldn't come back for their treats, I was determined to see my beautiful girl again if they did so.

So I scrunched myself into a ball near the sliding glass door and waited, chewing my nails and hoping the fondly-remembered smell of her miracle-sammies would cover my scent and push her to explore the backyard further.

As dusk turned to dark, Cherry and her two cubs slipped through the twilight, shadows of blackness melting in and out of the shrubbery along the hill, making their way ever so slowly and cautiously closer.

Afraid of scaring them off, I schlumped back inside, watching from the dark kitchen until blackness swallowed them, my heart and that empty area I fill with a passion for animals bursting at the seams.

Had I saved her?

No, even though I'll still happily claim that victory all day long (to the hubs at least.)

Cherry saved herself.

But I did give her lots of PB sammies and other eats coated in my particular brand of crazy love to help her along.

I guess that counts for something in the end, eh?

Who knows.

But let's go with that.

I am in the market for a new couch.
This one seems tasty!

NO
BEARS
PAST THIS POINT
This should clear up any
further misunderstandings

We appreciate you spending time with us and
the animals in *Don't Look a Gift Couch in the Mouth.*
Would you consider giving the book a review on your
venue of purchase? Your reviews help our authors and
their stories reach a wider audience.
Thank you so much in advance!

Well, that was
good for a laugh,
eh?
Next!
Whadya mean
we're out of stories?

Acknowledgments

I started this book many moons ago, and then life and a pandemic happened.

It got pushed to the back burner and all but forgotten, but in 2025 I dug it out of the trash-heap of my fondest animal memories and started plugging away at it again.

Special thanks to the guest authors who stuck with me and the book and allowed me to share their tales with the world at large: Christy Burbidge, Liz Casterlin, Lorena Estep, Joseph Horvath, Linda Kedersha, Martha Mosley, and Kuhu Roy.

Extra special thanks to Martha Mosley, who would be my favorite drill sergeant were I back in my military era. Martha is tough as nails but boasts a squishy center for the animals; she was exactly the tonic I needed to shove me off my comfort couch and back into the world of writing.

Extra extra special thanks to my hubby Joe, who I still hope never reads this book. Every comic writer needs a straight man for a foil, and Joe fits the role reluctantly yet to perfection. He really isn't an animal dude—gawd knows why we're together—but sometimes the results can be comic genius.

I'll always love ya, Bud. Thanks for 17 years (and counting?) of laughs.

About the Author

Tamira Thayne pioneered the anti-chaining movement in America as founder of the nonprofit organization Dogs Deserve Better. In 2011 her organization purchased Michael Vick's dogfighting compound and transformed it to a rescue and rehab center for chained dogs.

Tamira is the author of books including *It Went to the Dogs: How Michael Vick's Dogfighting Compound Became a Haven for Rescue Pups, Foster Doggie Insanity, Capitol in Chains, Smidgey Pidgey's Predicament,* and four other children's titles; she is the editor of *More Rescue Smiles and co-editor of Unchain My Heart* and *Rescue Smiles.*

Tamira's now embracing her retired and traveling era, which would be the most enjoyable of all the eras if it weren't for that pesky old age part. She currently resides in the West Virginia panhandle with Joe and cats Mori and Max.

Also from Author Tamira Thayne

More Rescue Smiles:
Best-Loved Animal Tales
of Resilience and Redemption

The heart of the animal rescue world lies in its stories—of freedom, of love, and of sacrifice by those who not only acknowledge but embrace the human-animal bond and its wondrous gifts.

In our second rescue story compilation, Who Chains You Books is pleased to share a glimpse into the emotional lives of animal rescuers and the living beings they hold close. Join us for another helping of heartwarming anecdotes, as Clancy triumphs, Tallulah escapes, Alex survives, and a host of other animals steal our hearts.

Through these stories, you'll get a behind-the-scenes look into the relationships between rescuers and not only dogs and cats, but horses, cows, pigs, birds, and even a ferret, in this delightful second installment of *Rescue Smiles.*

Read more and order from your favorite online or book outlets.

Also from Author Tamira Thayne

Also from Author Tamira Thayne